] CW00484828

**learning network
west**

A Whiting & Birch Ltd / SCA (Education) Co-Publication

Insights into Inspection:
The Regulation of Social Care

edited by

Roger Clough

Whiting and Birch Ltd

MCMXCIIII

Published by Whiting & Birch Ltd,
PO Box 872, , London SE23 3HL, England.
USA: Paul & Co, Publishers' Consortium Inc,
PO Box 442, Concord, MA 01742.
British Library Cataloguing in Publication Data.
A CIP catalogue record is available from
the British Library
ISBN 1 871177 79 0 (cased)
ISBN 1 871177 80 4 (limp)
Printed in England by Bourne Press, Poole

Contents

Acknowledgements

IT IS never easy to determine whom to thank. After all, it is hard to know from where we get our ideas, let alone what helps us find the energy to turn them into collections of words.

Nevertheless, all of us are aware that this book is the product of our work together in Cumbria Social Services. The setting up of the Inspectorate led to consideration of the nature of the work we had undertaken with all the obvious questions: what were we trying to do? for whose benefit? what systems were needed? and what resources? In addition, we had to work out how to liaise with different groups of people: providers of services, users of services, staff in the social services, staff from other agencies and councillors. We acknowledge the contribution that numerous people have made to our thinking and indeed to our practice.

In particular we wish to thank those with formal responsibility for the Inspectorate: Mary Styth and Anne Burns, the previous and current Chairs of Social Services; John Fletcher and Kay Whittle, the former and present Directors. Whatever else may emerge about inspection there is no doubt in our minds that the protection of the boundary that surrounds the inspection unit is fundamental to the integrity of the inspectorate and perhaps of the department. One of the strengths in Cumbria was that, whatever the pressures and however awkward might be the message from its findings, the inspectors worked under the assurance that their task was to report on daily life and practice as they found it. 'How can we know what needs to be done unless we have accurate pictures of how things are'?, successive chairs and directors said.

As inspectorate staff, we were a mixture of people with expertise in registration and inspection, and people new to the work. It has become a commonplace to acknowledge the significance of working in a context of change, 'Thriving on Chaos', in the words of Peters (1987). For all of us this was a period of significant change in our work lives on which we hope that we thrived. Certainly it was stimulating.

Individually, we are aware of people who have been significant for each of us in the production of this book. We have chosen not to list them but want to acknowledge help from Des Kelly who read the manuscript in draft and made suggestions about structure and detail.

Cumbria Social Services was our work base and the place where we began to think about the practice of inspection. This book could not have been written had we not come together. Nevertheless, we have written as individuals: the views are our own and should not be taken to be those of Cumbria County Council, its Social Services Committee nor of other individuals from the authority.

Roger Clough
Penrith, July 1994

Foreword

Roger Clough

AMBIVALENCE LIES at the heart of regulation. Inspections are good in abstract but an uncertain blessing in reality. We like the notion of inspections when we are consumers but see them as time consuming or restrictive when we are providers. Having recently had assessors from the Higher Education Funding Council inspecting the quality of our teaching at Lancaster University, I am only too aware of the volume of additional work created as the material was collected together in forms that 'they' wanted. There were pressures on staff as assessors observed teaching activities, bringing out internal questions as to how good the product really was. There were inevitable anxieties about the grading that the assessors would ascribe to different activities and the potential for competitiveness between individuals as to whose performance was best. Indeed, there was a wider uncertainty as to whether or not the 'inspectors' had the same criteria of quality as did internal staff. As in any organisation, staff were aware of their own shortcomings, some of which were declared to the assessors, some of which were not. Inevitably, some frustrations of the insiders (perhaps for not having made changes earlier), were projected on to the assessors. Rational selves may state that they are happy to be assessed at any time and that criticism is an important part of development; but there is an aspect of inspection which turns those inspected into children wanting the approval of adults. One of the hallmarks of successful inspection is that inspectors and inspected, aware of the underlying processes, are able to act as adults.

There is a measure of ambivalence within the market system. People are to be left free to produce the types and quality of goods and services which they want. The assumption is that the good producer will stay in business because goods and services are purchased and the bad producer will go out of business. But even the most ardent free marketeer no longer argues that there should be no checks and balances. It is accepted that it is not reasonable to allow some costs to lie where they fall; the argument becomes one about the degree or extent of the checks. Thus a government which established the current system for regulation of residential homes, schools and day care, becomes uneasy. Does the putting of the requirements into effect result in too much red tape, a focus on the 'wrong' factors or a standard that is too high and will drive out too many providers?

Regulation has become an integral component of the free market. Trading Standards Officers inspect premises to examine whether scales are accurate or pumps supply the stated amount of fuel. They inspect goods to check that they are safe and that they conform to the descriptions on the packet. In a recent case a company was prosecuted because there was less than the stated amount of fruit in a breakfast cereal. In other fields, the health and safety of people at work is inspected. Society is not prepared to rely on the integrity of the supplier of goods.

The market is not to be left without checks. Although the law has as a premise *caveat emptor*, 'let the buyer beware', with an expectation that the buyer must take steps to check out the quality of goods, there is an acknowledgement that buyers must also have protection. There are good reasons for this. Some factors are difficult for purchasers to be able to check. Thus, in choosing between different loaves of bread, it is important to know that the basic weight of a standard loaf is the same whatever the style of product. The need for protection becomes greater when the consumers of a service are vulnerable on account of their mental or physical state; these factors are compounded by any difficulty they may have in complaining or in taking their trade elsewhere. Regulation does not stop at inspection: there is legislation to protect the consumer and to provide redress.

A more recent development has been the extension of regulation into publicly provided services. It is no longer presumed that the fact of provision by a public body, such as a health authority or local authority, is sufficient guarantee of quality and integrity. The significant point is that there has been an increasing emphasis on a particular kind of regulation and accountability of public sector services. Previously, there had been an assumption (probably with a large measure of consensus) that the fact that public sector organisations were not profit making enterprises was in large measure sufficient protection from abuse. This was coupled with systems for scrutiny of activity. In local government this was achieved by the structure of democratically elected councillors who had oversight of and responsibility for service provision; other public sector organisations, such as health authorities, had people, elected or appointed, who were members of management boards.

There had been an assumption that abuse is most likely to occur when trying to make a profit. How far this had been valid is a matter for debate but either the political climate changed leading to a determination to take a more rigorous approach to publicly provided services or the extent of failings in the public sector became more widely recognised. The registration and inspection of residential homes for adults, children and young people and of day care for children under eight illustrate both of these trends. The private and voluntary sectors are allowed to expand provided that there are guarantees of adequacy; at the same time, and as part of the same policy changes, there are to be parallel inspections of local authority provided facilities.

James (1992) places the development of the drive to establish quality in the context of wider governmental policies: 'Over the decade of Thatcherism, central government declared the intention to work at best towards a free market in public service, at worst to an internal market or mixed economy' (p.45). She points out that setting and maintaining standards is central to privatisation and disaggregation. Indeed, because quality 'is apparently noncontroversial and feels good' (p.45) it encourages people not to think about the context of their activities. Inspection plays a part in wider systems, a point that will be picked up again in the final chapter.

This book is the product of the establishment and development of Cumbria Social Services Inspectorate. In its new format in Cumbria, the inspectorate came into existence in stages from October 1990. It had responsibility for the registration and/or inspection (dependent on statutory responsibilities) of day care for children under eight, of residential homes for adults, and of residential schools and children's homes. Further, there was an expectation that activities which are often described in terms such as 'quality assurance' or 'quality advice' would be undertaken, together with audit for the department of other functions of social service activity. This book is not a history, nor is it a description either of the process or the components of registration and inspection. Indeed, given the brief existence of social care inspectorates and the bombardment of proposals for change from the government, we are aware of the difficulty of letting go the material because of the urge to add yet another paragraph highlighting yet another change.

The context in which we were working and about which we are writing is that of inspection of social care services in England. There are differences in Northern Ireland, Scotland and Wales, as discussed by Brooke Ross (1993b, pp.3-6) in particular in relation to advisory committees. We think and hope that the core of the book, which is a reflection on the role and task of the inspectorates in the regulation of social care facilities, is relevant for social care inspection in these three countries; perhaps also there are themes which are pertinent to inspection outside social care. It is our view that good registration and inspection is dependent on an understanding and a management of the tensions and complexities inherent in the task. Thus the 'inspector', a word which we shall use as a shorthand for the person carrying out the functions of registration and inspection, has the task of assessing the quality of the provision and of reaching a judgement as to what should be done if there are deficits. The inspector has to take little (perhaps nothing) on trust but has to see the evidence. Yet, the inspector must try to establish relationships of trust with those being inspected. Relationships have to be established with providers without becoming so involved in their systems that it becomes impossible to take an independent judgement.

We hope that the values which we specified and to which we subscribed will become apparent. Some details from our documentation are set out in the Appendix. Establishing new units with new functions is likely to create excitement and, hopefully, enthusiasm. We were determined to demonstrate that 'inspection' is an activity that requires the skills of good social work and social care: assessment based on theory and knowledge; listening to different parties, all of whom have legitimate interests; reviewing options, based on knowledge of legislation and procedures and the assessment of the provision; exercise of judgement concerning the assessment and the action to be taken; assessment of risk; liaison with other professionals; specification of procedures, guidelines and standards, together with the provision of information about them; making public, as appropriate, the findings; at ease with, but not excited by, the exercise of authority. In our view these are professional skills. It is possible to learn skills and improve performance, for example in the way in which options are examined. Nevertheless, the 'skill' element must not blind us to the fact that judgements are not made in a vacuum. An inspector must set what is seen against a notion, as we discuss in Chapter Six, of what is a good enough service. That picture of the good enough service is not drawn from scientific manuals. Built up from whatever components, tested in whatever way, it is based on moral reasoning (Thorpe, 1994).

Inspection as an activity is one of intervention. Let us accept that in a given situation, it is acknowledged that practice in a particular place is inadequate; a decision still has to be reached as to whether particular types of enforcement action should be carried out. The responsibility of the regulator in taking that action is significant. As an inspector, I have been involved in decisions which matter for the users and providers of services: at an extreme, should the inspectorate present a case why an establishment should close? As an outsider, I have heard from providers in other authorities than the one where I worked of the trauma of inspections and investigations. My point is not whether or not inspectors made good or bad judgements in those cases; I do not have the information for that. Rather, it is that there are other perspectives than those of the inspection unit. Inevitably I ask myself, as colleagues in Cumbria will have done on other occasions: 'Did we get the process and the judgement right?'

Inspectorates, as other organisations, should set out their value bases. This is useful for internal staff and allows examination by others. However, such statements never prescribe what is to be done; rather they set out the principles which are taken into account when working out what to do, for example 'that the overriding responsibility is to the welfare of current and future users of services'.

We are not attempting a detailed comparison of the functions of social care inspection with other related activities, such as child protection, adult protection, policing, or other inspectorates, fascinating and important as that may be. As with much other current activity in social services departments, there are questions as to the sort of people that make the best social care inspectors: are they to be specialists in inspection or in social care? what qualifications and training do they need? There is a concern as to whether staff will be able to move from one type of work to another, indeed, whether inspection will be regarded as mainstream, a valuable post for a manager to gain understanding and knowledge, or a backwater. That, as is said, is another story and perhaps another book. This story starts from the feelings of being inspected and inspecting, and tries to find the clues which explain the process. It attempts to reveal insights on inspection, rather than to set out the process of how to inspect, as would a manual.

The language used to describe people and situations is significant. As we all know, new words are used in attempts to avoid the negative connotations of particular phrases which label people or from a desire to emphasise different aspects of a role. It is easy to see why officer in charge has been dropped. In the process we sometimes find that a core characteristic has been hidden or lost; in the case of the shift from officer in charge, the reality of the power inherent in the post may be hidden. The debates are familiar about what to term the people with whom social workers work. Ward (1993, p.xii) states that he prefers client to the alternatives. Social care is as subject to current culture as other trades. British Rail talk of customers rather than passengers. We are faced with a cluster of words used to describe people and the places where they live, work or visit: customers, stakeholders, users, interested parties, providers and purchasers as well as the longer standing resident, manager, proprietor, home, school, establishment, institution, facility, playgroup, childminder. There is not space here to examine the implications of these different perspectives though they need to be understood in the context of wider movements and trends.

Writing about individuals, persons and people is our preference but we have to find ways to distinguish people doing different jobs and in different roles. A further point is that there are times when, to avoid lengthy sentences, we want single words or short phrases to describe all the people who are subject to inspection, all the people in residential or day care who are the service users, clients or customers or all the places which are regulated by social care inspectorates. For variety we use different phrases but have tried to draw attention to occasions when the specific use of a word is intended to highlight a particular characteristic. Thus we use: resident to refer to a person living in a residential home; service user about people who live in residential homes or schools or attend day care; managers at times to include owners as well as managers; establishment or facility to cover all the places which are inspected. Our terms are intended to be neutral, although we know they are part of wider systems and cultures. We are aware that some people do not like being called resident and that others do not understand service user. Indeed, if we were to extend our discussion, we would examine the reasons why some people wish to describe the people who carry out the task of regulation as quality assurance officers; we have stuck to the word inspector because we think this is fundamental to the role, though for brevity we use it to refer to people who register as well as inspect.

Once upon a time there were no inspectors of these facilities. And then from the nineteenth century there has been a developing function of inspection. Is this the story of the inspector as wolf, huffing and puffing to blow the house down, with all the questions that might be asked as to whether the house should be blown down or could have been saved, and whether the wolf had enough huff or puff? Or is it the story of the inspector as woodcutter who saves the vulnerable Red Riding Hood from the jaws of the wolf, dressed up in staff clothing?

Fairy tales tell of the inner worlds of hopes and dreams, fears and fantasies. Regulation touches deep seated feelings from childhood about adequacy, approval, self sufficiency, secrets and guilt. We have tried both to reflect on the task and acknowledge the feelings generated by registration and inspection.

One

The context of inspection

Roger Clough

INTRODUCTION

REGISTRATION AND inspection, the regulatory activities of social care, are likely to be regarded as necessary evils rather than as good in themselves. They exist because of frailty. All interested groups have ambivalent or even contradictory feelings to regulation: those being inspected, service users and providers, for different reasons approve of inspection and find it a nuisance; those who establish regulation and those who oversee it feel the same; it is perhaps surprising to become aware that those who carry out regulation also have the same tensions. The obvious but critical concern is how you ensure compliance with stated standards. Once it is acknowledged in relation to certain social care activities that there has to be some regulation because it is not acceptable to leave the costs of inefficiency or malpractice to fall where they lie, the issue becomes that of specifying and establishing a system.

THE NATURE OF REGULATION IN PUBLIC AND INDEPENDENT SECTORS

The idea of regulation is easy to adopt. The problems emerge immediately implementation is started. The first set of issues surrounds the setting of standards: what are the minimally acceptable standards? what are the crucial factors to include in the specification? is it possible to specify the details that will provide evidence of what are often regarded as intangibles?

Secondly, there are issues about the amount of regulation that is necessary to do the job. Everyone is likely to start from the premise of minimum intervention. The dilemma is, 'What is the minimum intervention which will achieve the desired result?'. Is there a link between the number of inspections and the effectiveness of regulation? Similarly, what is the nature of the difference created by having two inspectors on a visit rather than one, or by spending two days on a visit rather than a half day? Given that it is possible that you may not get eight times as much useful information from a two day visit by two inspectors rather than from a half day inspection by one person, is there any knowledge of the difference in potential?

The third variable is the nature of the authority to be allocated to the inspector. What power is to be given to an inspector to take action when there are judged to be concerns?

All of these dimensions take us back to the dilemma posed at the beginning of the chapter, the dilemma that lies at the heart of regulation: regulation is both wanted and is feared. It is important to recognise that both attitudes are appropriate, for there is a danger of getting into one camp or another and failing to recognise the tension. Will regulation result in a killing of difference and creativity? Will the inspector become too powerful, a rampant beast interfering in matters that should not be her or his concern? The standard joke amongst local authority provider staff that before long there will be more inspectors than there are practitioners captures this anxiety. At the heart of the question is the long standing philosophical and practical issue. if guards are needed to protect, who guards the guards?

The same concern is present whether the guards exist to protect people, property or standards.

In August 1993 the Department of Health (1993c) issued a letter stating:

> ...the Prime Minister has declared his intention to reduce the regulatory burden on business. We have been asked to assess the cost of regulation on business, to consider whether there is a continued need for regulation, and whether the system can be improved to reduce the burden in any way.

The letter included the significant phrase, 'Even if there is a continuing need for the Registered Homes Act, it may be possible to identify ways in which the burden it imposes on business could be reduced'.

Considerable concern about the proposals was expressed by voluntary organisations, local authority associations and professional bodies. As a consequence there was an attempt to distance the government from the letter, by stressing the consultative nature of the letter and the government's wish to ensure high quality care. Nevertheless, the letter is a fine illustration of the government's uncertainty and ambivalence to regulation. At stake is how to carry out the dual function of freeing business from 'unnecessary' administrative requirements and ensuring high quality, or at the least acceptable, provision. The letter had specifically mentioned the possibility that the Registered Homes Act might not be needed. Ill advised as the letter was, the issue of what goes on under the guise of regulation is important. In Chapter Seven I shall be considering one of the same issues as the letter writer: 'whether any requirements are out of proportion to the risks which they are seeking to redress'.

Within two and a half years, the government shifted to and fro as it faced the contradictory pressures from varying bodies: it introduced new regulatory procedures, criticised the structures it had introduced, tried to respond to people attacking the new system and subsequently to those defending it, and wrote revised procedures.

The crux is that regulation necessarily results in intervention. Consequently, the nature of that intervention is subject to question and challenge. The argument put forward against the specifics of registration nearly always runs as follows: 'Regulation is a good thing; however, this specific requirement is unnecessary because...'. The probability is that the challenge will be put in terms of political bias, focus on unimportant detail or lack of understanding by inspectorates (whether of business, education or social care). The difficulty for anyone who wants to enter the debate is to determine the basis for the setting of standards. In part, specification is wanted because that leads to knowledge, and the knowledge is power, allowing questioning, whether of particular standards or of comparability between establishments. Yet, in part specification is disliked because it sets precise details. The case against specification is that leaving matters to the discretion of inspectors results in greater flexibility. An additional view that often accompanies this perspective is that it is obvious when an establishment is terrible and, therefore, the detailed setting of standards is unnecessary and restricting.

There are good reasons why inspectors must set precise standards. First, they should not risk relying on their own assumptions, which may have elements of prejudice and stereotyping. Secondly, there should be consultation about the components of good practice. Thirdly, in presenting their views about adequacy and inadequacy, inspectorate staff must set out evidence which will stand up to scrutiny.

The government, as everybody else with an interest, has to define what it wants from regulation. Perhaps we need a dictum to match the weary political comments that 'If you cannot stand the heat, you should get out of the kitchen' or 'You cannot make an omelette without breaking eggs'. The dictum for inspection would be, 'You cannot find out what is going on beneath the surface without disturbing the covering'. Regulation requires metaphorically and, at times directly, that cupboard doors are opened, carpets are lifted and lights are shone into corners.

Assaults on people in public buildings, schools, hospitals or residential homes, result in cries for better security, whether by TV surveillance or security personnel. Tax, pension or share fraud lead to demands for bodies to oversee standards. And of course legislation exists to protect and take action. Underlying the debates on any of these topics will be the concerns as to whether greater regulation will achieve the desired result and whether the outcome is worth the cost. Indeed, there will be people who argue that regulation makes people less trustworthy: providers learn to rely on the regulator to impose standards; they take less individual responsibility; their task becomes that of convincing the regulator.

Regulation illustrates also the debate about prescription and discretion. Again, the issues appear over the spectrum of welfare services and beyond: are welfare benefits more appropriately matched to individuals if the person responsible for their administration has discretion? Alternatively, does discretion lead to inappropriate power and idiosyncrasy? Similar issues emerge in the administration of justice: is sentencing better or worse (in whatever terms these are defined) when magistrates or judges have discretion?

Thus it becomes apparent that questions about systems, organisational structures and accountability should not be regarded as unique to social care regulation. The same controversies and dilemmas exist in other settings. However, the dominant issue in any field at a particular time may differ from that in another, which will lead to different imperatives. For example, in one area the critical current issue may be to ensure the efficiency of the inspecting body while in another area the drive might be to establish impartiality. The chosen structures will reflect this.

The government chose in the early 1990s to remove the authority for inspection of local authority schools from the education departments of local authorities and pass it to inspectors licensed by the Department for Education. Indeed, so determined was the government to ensure that power moved away from the local authority (whether to the Department for Education, and so ministers, or to schools is debatable) that early drafts of legislation allowed schools to choose their own licensed inspectors. By contrast, there has been no debate about the location of trading standards departments in local authorities: again, conjecture may lead us to consider whether this was because the nature of what they inspect is thought to be harder edged, and thus less open to variation and to the ideological framework of inspectors, or because trading standards officers are so well established that the government chose not to intervene.

Of course, some imperatives at any one time may override others: thus a drive to move services outside the control of local authorities may result in this being adopted as the system for an inspectorate even though there are thought to be good reasons for locating it in a local authority; or, as seems the case for social care regulation, the reverse may be the case. Alternatively a government may create more stringent regulatory systems even though it starts from being committed to decreasing regulation, because of powerful public concern on a particular matter.

THE ORGANISATION AND LOCATION OF SOCIAL CARE REGULATION

Decisions on the organisational structures, the authority and the specifications for social care inspectorates have to be seen in the context of the these wider issues. Thus a government which was committed to regulate social care more rigorously (evidenced in 1989 with the Children Act and in 1990 with the NHS and Community Care Act) gave the responsibility for regulation of residential care homes, residential schools and day care for children under eight to the local authority. It should be noted that the guidance stated that the local authority had to ensure that the service was provided, commenting that such units might be provided by the social services department, elsewhere in the local authority or purchased from an outside body. But the guidance also recognised that the most obvious location was within the social services department because of the potential to build on existing expertise and because such units could be managed more easily without creating additional management systems.

One of the key differences from education is that social care inspectorates have responsibility for the registration of certain independent sector facilities: education inspectors only inspect. The act of registration leads to the power to initiate proceedings to cancel registration.

INSPECTION AT ARMS LENGTH

Locating such units within local authorities left them open to the charge that they would not have sufficient independence to inspect local authority and independent sector facilities in an even handed way. Therefore one of the current catch words, 'arms-length', came into play. The units were to be at 'arms length' from the managers providing the local authority residential and day care services. In effect, this has meant within most authorities that the person responsible for the inspection unit is accountable either to the Director of Social Services or to a Deputy Director, the guidance preferring the accountability to be to the Director. This separation of functions within one organisation is not unique to the inspectorate since the purchasing arm of the social services department is also to be at arms length from the provider section.

Any chosen organisational system has the potential to resolve some dilemmas but not others. Being termed 'arms length' but managed by the Director of Social Services is in many ways a strange organisational system. The Director is responsible both for the arms length integrity of the inspection unit and for the provision and purchasing which may be the subject of inspection. The head of the inspection unit is accountable to the Director in the sense that her/his work is overseen by the Director. Consequently, the Director, as any line manager in other settings, may, indeed should, comment on the quality of the inspection work. The Director's managerial responsibility for the inspectorate should include: the setting of standards, the priorities of the inspectorate, the quality of the work of inspectorate staff and the production of reports.

What is required from both parties (Director and Head of Unit) is primacy of role. The Director will only manage properly the responsibilities for different sections with their potential conflicts of interest if the overall task can be broken down into discrete sections and if the role drives the task. Of course life is not that explicit nor straightforward. For example, a report of an inspection into a local authority residential home setting out major problems might be seen by the Director. Examples of the sort of questions which the Director as line manager should be asking of the Chief Inspector are: 'Is there evidence for the conclusions? Does the balance of the report seem appropriate to the material? Is the language used in the report clear and of an appropriate weight for the statements made? Are the conclusions of the report too hidden or unnecessarily (perhaps inappropriately) blazoned on the page?'

It is worth noting also that the same issues have to be considered in relation to independent sector provision. The questions have a different edge or consequence but remain significant for judgements have to be made about what is to be included in reports, knowing that the information will become public. Other questions could be added to those above: 'Is there a duty on the inspectorate to report on particular matters? Is it in the public interest for the matter to be included in the report? What account has to be taken of the effect publicity may have on the commercial viability of the establishment? How far do previous judgements about the place influence what is reported?'. Reporting on independent and publicly provided services raises similar issues. For the present discussion, the critical factor is the way in which the potential conflict of interests of the managers of inspection units is handled.

For example, it is difficult both for the Head of the Unit

and for the Director to be clear whether a question from the Director as to the appropriateness of making in a report a particular statement about a local authority facility stems from the wish not to expose the poor performance for which, ultimately, she/he is responsible, or from an even handed question which would be asked of any facility. Conversely, a Head of Unit might avoid writing something critical because of a realisation that the consequent publicity will cause difficulties for the authority for which he/she works. The nub of the issue is that systems do not guarantee integrity, though many of the assumptions of guidance notes presumes that it is specific structures which will solve these type of issues.

In fact 'arms lengthness' and integrity are negotiated between two individuals. In Cumbria the Chief Inspector, as other second tier officers, had responsibility for managing a section which was not and could not have been seen in detail by the Director. The tension in roles was resolved formally by an explicit statement that reports from the inspectorate would go out under the name of the Chief Inspector, not the Director, and no report would be published by the inspectorate unless the Chief Inspector was satisfied with its contents. Such 'rules' do not dispense with the tension, but they play a part in the way in which individuals with particular functions deal with the internal conflict. In the end each individual has to be confident in her/his ability to determine the action to be taken by the responsibility of the role, and also has to be confident in the reliability of the other person to do the same.

There are considerable advantages in the inspectorate being part of a local authority. The Department of Health as part of the case for recommending that inspectorates be placed in social services departments, cited the expertise of existing staff within social services departments and the efficiency of using social services department management structures. In addition, the inspectorate is able to acquire knowledge of social services department developments and to influence them. Such opportunities produce similar tensions between section heads as those already referred to between directors and heads of units: at issue is the nature of the involvement and influence of inspectorate with provider and purchasing sections and vice versa. The danger at one end of a continuum is that the inspectorate might be so influential in a particular development that it would find itself in due course inspecting an activity in which it had too much investment to be able to take a disciplined view of performance. At the other end of that continuum is an inspectorate that is so out of touch with what is happening in its own authority that local authority providers or purchasers produce standards for services which are in direct conflict with those of the inspection unit.

However well defined and appropriate is the working out of 'being at arms length' within the department, those outside may consider that there is bound to be collusion between those with distinct responsibilities. Owners of independent sector residential homes in Cumbria often voiced the charge that the inspectorate was party to decisions made by the newly formed purchasing unit. 'You must have known that they (the purchasers) had decided on this or that' or 'You are not going to tell me that you weren't a part of such and such a decision!', inspectorate staff would be told. Stating that one did not know was presumed to be a lie or ineptitude.

A further advantage for an inspectorate in being part of a local authority is that there is greater potential for staff movement to and from the inspectorate. Inspection within social services in its current scope is new and that there is no certainty yet as to the training and professional base of inspectors; there is a possibility that inspection will be a cul-de-sac: a job that is attractive in salary terms when entering but is separated from other jobs, so making it difficult for inspectors to leave. The danger is greater if inspection were to become an activity outside the main core of social service activity, and a job which is not thought to have skills valuable for future management.

OFFICERS, COUNCILLORS, POLITICAL PARTIES AND EVEN HANDEDNESS

The issue faced by a Director of how to manage the distinct roles of being responsible for the provision of services, for the purchasing of services and for the integrity of arms length inspection exists also for councillors. Councillors have to oversee and support the ability of the inspectorate to report without fear or favour and, in fulfilling that function, have to be able to question and direct policy. Yet, sitting on other committees, they have to receive the reports which may criticise the services which they are expected to oversee, support, question and direct. They too are subject to feelings at times that it would be easier if the inspectorate would fudge its findings.

The topic of even-handedness is discussed in greater detail in the next section. The significant structural factors are that the inspectorate:

1. in nearly all cases is under the management of the Director of Social Services;
2. is subject to review by the Chief Executive of the local authority;
3. is subject to oversight and review by councillors.

Perhaps the most important point is that each of these groups has an interest in: i) the provision of services; ii) the purchase of services from a variety of providers including those from its own organisation; and iii) even handed inspection of both its own directly provided services and those of other providers. In all of this, the stance taken by the different parties towards the notion of a variety of providers, what has become known as the mixed economy of welfare, is significant.

A further perspective on the tension for and between individuals emerges from the roles and jobs of different groups of councillors and officers. These are:

1. 'senior' social services councillors with responsibilities for the whole range of social service activity (purchasing, provision and inspection); this equates with the tensions

of role for the Director and applies particularly to the Chair of the Committee and to party spokespersons;

2. social services councillors with primary responsibilities for functions other than inspection;
3. social services councillors with primary responsibility for inspection;
4. senior officers with responsibilities for the whole range of social service activity (purchasing, provision and inspection); the Director may be the only officer in this category;
5. social services officers with primary responsibilities for functions other than inspection;
6. social services officers with primary responsibility for inspection;
7. officers and councillors from outside the social services department or committee (such as the fire service) who have an interest in the regulatory activity because inspection draws on resources from their areas of interest.

It is important to remember that tasks and roles rarely are divided as neatly as this may suggest. People may be members of groups in which they represent the interests of their section but have a collective responsibility for general management decisions.

The question with which we are faced in attempting to consider whether inspectorates operate even handedly is the same as that which exits for different providers: it is a question of trust. Heads of residential schools, as will be shown in Chapter Two, think, indeed fear, that inspectorates hold fundamentally divergent views to themselves about the appropriateness of fee paying, boarding education. It is as if they were being inspected by their enemies. An issue of the same order underpins other inspections: are interested parties, whether called customers or stakeholders, able to have confidence in the capacity and the integrity of the inspectors? Arising from this, the view that inspectorates have, or indeed are thought to have, may seem the key reason behind the stance taken in an inspection. 'They were out to get us', is the statement that summarises this position.

Councillors are central to this dimension because, in contrast to officers, in political groups they state their opinions on exactly these matters. They may declare whether or not they support independent sector (in particular private) or public (local authority) provision. Two comments typify this: 'It's in the private sector where they're out for profit that the worst abuses occur'; or, alternatively, 'Local authority staff have been protected from the real world for too long - it's time some efficiency was brought into the sector'. Of course not all political parties have taken fixed stances on public or private provision but many have, and presumptions are made about the views of many more. Once their positions are publicised, what confidence will providers from the different sectors have in the impartial oversight of a political group which has expressed opposition to its particular type of provision?

The assumption behind such questions is that people operate on a uni-dimensional model: if someone does not approve of a certain type of provision she/he will act in all circumstances to disadvantage that service. In reality life is far more complex for individuals have a cluster of values. Thus it is possible for councillors to state in public their preferences as to which organisations should provide services, but also to insist that an inspectorate be allowed, indeed supported, in its independence. This position is akin to that discussed in relation to the Director where the primacy of the role and of the process may hold sway over other interests.

There are two key factors in whether inspections are as even handed as is possible within the constraints of the legislation: the first is the inspectors themselves (their skills, integrity, ability to hold to their core task); the second is the context in which they are allowed to operate - does the unit feel confident that senior management and councillors support the view that inspections are to be even handed although such even handedness may not be comfortable? There is an important interplay between the inspectorate on the one hand and the councillors and officers on the other. At issue is how an understanding is reached of what appropriate independence means in practice. Thus, inspectors may be aware of the statements of councillors about public or independent sector provision, or, as others, may presume that they know the opinions of councillors. The extent to which inspectors will act in an even handed way depends on the individual inspector's integrity and style, on the extent to which the Chief Inspector ensures that boundaries to protect staff are maintained, on the management styles and systems of the Director as well as on the integrity and style of individual councillors.

Councillors carry out their responsibilities in different ways but it is significant for inspectorates that one of these ways is to visit facilities which the local authority directly provides. This means that as part of their oversight they may visit the same establishments which the inspectors are inspecting. How does an inspector deal with a consequent complaint from a councillor? Indeed, the inspector is further vulnerable: as anyone else, a councillor may look at the publicly available report and inform the inspectorate that the report misses important matters and, indeed, makes an incorrect assessment. Inspection units have to find ways of agreeing procedures with councillors which will allow the inspectorate to take on board questions and complaints, to ensure proper oversight by councillors of the work of the unit but also to guarantee that the inspection unit will not be subject to improper influence. The reports have to be written without fear or favour. This is a specific aspect of the location of power amongst and between officers and councillors. The power of influence is related both to formal role and to individual style and is best seen as a negotiation. (Clough, 1990, pp.59-61, 78-82, 167-70)

Nor should the political complexion of the local authority be presumed to indicate the attitude of councillors to the operation of the inspectorate. Councillors differ not only in whether or not they believe in private or public provision. They also take various positions on the style of relationship between councillor and officer: in some authorities it is expected that councillors will be involved in day to day decisions; in others, the expectation is that the councillors main task is to set policy and then to leave officers to implement it. This is an example of the situation that has always faced councillors and officers: councillors have to oversee the work of the officers, and be able to ask questions about the affairs of individual constituents without improperly interfering with the judgement of the officers, whether about allocation of resources or recommendations in reports.

The effect of this on inspectors is to be found in day to day events as well as in policy decisions. The group of councillors who want to be involved in day to day decisions have to find a way to inform officers of their concern and yet to leave officers to get on with the resolution. The fundamental point is that, whatever the style of the councillor, the responsibility for managing services rests with officers. In this inspection provides as stark an illustration as does child protection: councillors have the responsibility neither for deciding which children should be placed on a register of children at risk nor for determining the content of an inspection report. They are responsible for the oversight of both services.

There are potential dangers for inspectorate staff in the relationship between officers and inspectors: for the Chief Inspector, there is the risk that the impartiality of the inspectorate will be put at risk, that policy decisions will favour one sector rather than another and that it will become impossible to ensure that reports and action are produced without fear or favour; for the individual inspector, there is the worry that the councillor will visit a home or day care establishment, will take a different view than the inspector of the quality and expect the inspector to revise the report.

Another group which might exercise undue influence is the providers. It is possible for inspection units, stressing partnership, to become so caught up in establishing relationships with providers that they are unable to determine their own inspectorate view either of the standards which should be set or of the judgements that should be reached on particular facilities. It would be easy for collusive relationships to develop between inspectors and providers from the local authority or the independent sectors.

HOW FAIR ARE THE SYSTEMS?

The test of even-handedness is whether inspection units behave in the same way to all providers, regardless of whether they are private, voluntary or local authority. It would be reasonable to expect that this would mean that the inspectorate would establish one set of standards and procedures and adopt them for all its interactions with service providers. The fact that this cannot be so is a source of frustration not only for independent sector owners but also for inspectors. The most important difference is that independent sector providers of residential homes (whether for children or adults) have to be registered before they are allowed to operate; local authority facilities do not have to register. The fact that all facilities have to be inspected against the same standards does not compensate for the different base position. (Residential schools, whoever the provider, do not have to register with the local authority although they are subject to inspection; local authority provided day care for children under eight does have to be registered in the same circumstances as independent sector providers).

Independent sector providers may not trade without first being registered. Thus, they have to go through a process of approval before they are allowed to operate. There are consequent further distinctions in terms of powers available to inspectors: if dissatisfied with a registered, independent sector provider the inspectorate may take action to cancel registration, to vary conditions of registration or to require compliance within a stated period. By contrast, with the local authority home, the inspectorate may report on its shortcomings including commenting to the Director and councillors, but the inspectorate has no authority to take action against the home if nothing is done to rectify the problem. This arises not from the wish of inspectorates to treat people differently; indeed, some authorities have laid down procedures for the way in which they will try to establish equivalence, as will be illustrated in Chapter Seven. The legislation has determined that the two sectors have different systems of approval.

Criticisms of the inspection system emerge from different parties: some people argue that inspectorates themselves act in ways which treat different providers unequally; others contend that through no fault of the inspectorates, statutes have determined that there will be differential treatment of different providers. In brief the criticisms may be grouped under the following headings:

1. that different standards are used at inspections;
2. that subsequent inspection reports demand higher standards (or judge more harshly) in one sector than in another;
3. that the action taken by inspectorates differs between sectors.

The fundamental difference in structure ensures that inspectorates cannot be even handed. They may work very hard to inspect against the same standards and issue reports which are of similar nature. But they have different authority to take action. This is not rectified by individual authorities trying to be 'even handed'. The Department of Health (1994c) emphasises the obligations on inspection units. In relation to follow up action the circular states:

> The same requirements to respond to inspection reports should apply equally to providers in all sectors, *taking account of any necessary differences between services.* Mechanisms need to exist when local authority managers do not respond appropriately. (5.7. p.30, my italics)

It is as if the phrase even handed has been developed by the Department of Health to mean 'the creation of special procedures to get as near to equivalence as possible in a situation where the legislation has created fundamental differences which we will pretend have no significance'. I do not dispute the value of trying to establish equivalent procedures. The key point is that official guidance ignores the importance of legislative distinctions which remain one of the biggest reasons cited by independent sector managers for their claim that local authority homes have preferential treatment.

The disparity in registration and consequent action remains. There are claims that inspectors treat providers differently. The information offered nearly always is anecdotal, the stories that people tell of how they have been treated more harshly than similar places elsewhere. It must be remembered that this is not just a view held by independent sector providers; local authority staff, as will be discussed in Chapter Two, similarly consider that they get worse treatment than do equivalent private and voluntary homes.

One element of this is common to any occasion when people are caught out or shown in reports to need to improve their performance. People stopped by police for speeding often acknowledge that they were in breach of regulations. Nevertheless, there is a feeling of injustice: 'Why me?', they ask, 'others were going faster'. Indeed, motoring organisations support cameras which will record speeding on the grounds that motorists will know that all are being treated equally. So it is probable that, were there no variations in procedures required by statutes, managers would still think that other homes were being treated more leniently. The significance is that because there are distinct procedures, it is possible to project those feelings of being hard done by on to another sector.

Even handedness requires consistency: managers want to be confident that they are being treated reasonably and fairly in comparison with others. Studies of analyses by inspectors of different homes have questioned the extent to which different inspectors are likely to produce similar reports on the same establishment. Gibbs and Sinclair (1992a) writing of inspectors assessing homes according to a number of 'evaluative items' in check lists comment on an 'apparently low degree of agreement' which 'does not provide reliable backing for tribunal decisions'.

> Any quality control system based on inspection is likely to require an inspector to assess whether a home is satisfactory in certain respects. If the reliability of such judgements is low, this casts doubts on an apparently essential element of arms' length inspection (p.114).

They continue (pp.119-124) by arguing that it is possible to improve consistency by establishing good check lists (which are to be used as a starting point rather than absolute indicators) and by examining the philosophical base. In particular, if the focus of inspection is on what needs to be improved, rather than an attempt at assessing quality, there is far greater consistency between inspectors.

The reason for this probably lies more in the nature of the task than in preferential treatment for one sector rather than another.

At the heart of inspection is an analysis of life in one facility set against what is judged to be 'good practice'. The picture of good practice must itself be drawn from views of the factors which comprise a good life. Thus, when inspectorates examine the extent to which individuals have choice, they are making a judgement not only that choice is important but also of the types of choice which are significant. It is no wonder that Gibbs and Sinclair found that individual inspectors tended to focus on different factors. Inspectorates may reduce such inconsistency by detailed specification, and by training. In addition, they may use paired inspections as a way of a) highlighting the differences in focus of inspectors, b) monitoring the work of individuals and c) establishing a common and consistent approach. My point is that in examining consistency it is important to be aware of background factors which lead those being inspected to think that others are being treated more favourably and which lead inspectors to find it hard to establish consistency.

I know of no studies which have attempted to validate the hypothesis that inspection units inspect one sector more leniently than another. Yet the statements that this is the case are numerous. In Cumbria there were statements (allegations from the inspection unit's perspective) that local authority homes were given preferential treatment in what was reported at inspections. Yet critical reports of local authority homes which were publicly available would in a different context be used by the same lobby to present a case that local authority homes had been shown by the reports to be in need of substantial improvements. These were contrasted with reports on particular independent sector home which did not require improvements. The argument of the inspectorate was that like had to be compared to like: there were seriously critical reports of independent sector homes and of local authority homes. In each case it was made clear that action was necessary; at subsequent inspections there would be reviews of what had been done. It was at that stage that difference would come in, although as has been noted, procedures were introduced to establish equivalency.

The structures in which inspectorates are located within social services could lead to improper interference from either the Director or councillors. As I have already stated, there is nothing other than hearsay and anecdote to allow any judgements to be made on whether the structures are leading to inspectorates being unable to carry out their job. There is evidence that inspectorates have had an impact on both local authority and independent sector services, though it is not possible to gauge whether this means that they are able to work appropriately in the present system, or that there is improper influence on inspectorates. I have argued that the location of inspectorates within social services departments can work and that, currently, the advantages of this system outweigh the disadvantages. It is apparent also that the risk to the integrity of inspectorates comes from providers as well as Director or councillors.

It becomes clear that inspectors are bound to be faced with different groups wishing to influence their decisions. That is proper. The task for all interested parties is to find a way of defining appropriate influence. Whatever the structure, it is essential that all with an interest in inspection are aware of the need to guarantee that the boundary around the inspectorate properly protects the units from interference in judgements. Further, it is worth repeating that structures and systems on their own do not produce the desired results of integrity of inspectorates: in any system there has to be negotiation between individuals. Other structures would create their own sets of problems.

HEALTH AND SOCIAL SERVICES INSPECTORATES

There has been little mention so far of the parallel responsibilities of health authorities for the inspection of nursing homes. Some residential homes are dually registered with social services and health authorities in that the home (or parts of it) are registered both for nursing and residential care. The distinction between residential care and nursing care on which the two registration categories are defined is imprecise. The rule of thumb that a place is to be defined as a nursing home when a resident requires the attendance of nursing as distinct from care staff for more than occasional help, inevitably is open to differing interpretations. The importance of the distinction is embodied in the fact that it is an offence for the owner of a residential care home to look after someone who ought to be in a nursing home, though the reverse is not the case. A nursing home has to employ a qualified nurse at all times in recognition of the complexity of working with 'nursing home' residents.

It does not need much imagination to see that owners may try to drive a wedge between the two authorities, arguing that the standards required by the two are very different. There are many fewer nursing than residential care homes for adults so health authority inspectorates are much smaller. They are also subject to different management systems: there has not been the same emphasis on health authority inspectorates being at arms length from provider or purchaser units, perhaps on the grounds that there are very few health authority run nursing homes and so far less potential for a conflict of interests. Of course the oversight of the health authority inspection unit also differs from that within the local authority: the health authority inspection unit reports eventually to the health authority, which has different structures and responsibilities to the local authority.

In some areas health and local authority inspectorates have found ways to merge their units, either by one authority contracting for its work to be carried out by the other or by the two units working from the same base, with an agreement about joining in each others' work. In these circumstances, typically staff continue to work for their respective authorities though there are occasions when they move to new employers. There are contextual factors which influence decisions about such mergers and liaison: the extent to which the boundaries of one authority are coterminous with those of the other; whether the local authority inspection unit has responsibility solely for adult residential provision or also for children's services (children's homes, residential schools and day care of children under eight) since the health authority inspection unit has no responsibility parallel to that for services for children.

This debate is an example of wider and recurring debates about organisations: is collaboration best achieved by merger, by exhortation or by procedure? There is an obvious case for close working arrangements between health and local authority inspectorates; the systems in any locality which will best establish such working arrangements will vary. Difficulties may be overcome by liaison as well as by merger. The temptation to reorganise to cope with current problems is generally one to be avoided unless there are overriding benefits. Challis (1990) shows that reorganisations in social services departments leave staff continually under pressure to cope with change for minimal benefit. Her message is in effect saying, 'Don't reorganise unless, following analysis, you judge it essential'. She cites three 'things to remember':

1. that no reorganisation is going to solve all the problems which SSDs (social services departments) experience, and
2. that our search for the desirable must always be tempered with an understanding of what is probable rather than what is possible, and
3. whatever we do will have consequences in addition to the ones we intend (p.148).

My point is that the critical factor is to be sure of what it is that is desired before reorganising. Whether or not the desirable is achievable, goals such as common standards or joining together in inspections may be better accomplished through co-operation than restructuring. Brooke Ross (undated) sets out some of the advantages of joint working and the theme is pursued in this book in Chapter Seven in relation to systems.

OVERSIGHT OF REGULATION

The expectation or need for local authority inspectorates to work with health authority inspectorates arises from the fact that both groups have a direct responsibility for regulatory activities in similar types of residential homes. The issue of oversight arises for other reasons: once it is determined that an organisation is to carry out registration and inspection there are consequent concerns about the power that is given to that body. So in diverse settings people want to know to whom the police or inspectors of prisons are to be accountable.

The same applies to inspection units. Who is to decide if their interventions are necessary and effective or inappropriate and burdensome? The issue is compounded by the realisation that people will use the same evidence to draw contrary conclusions. Thus, information that heads of schools find the inspectorates to be interfering and a nuisance will lead some to consider that they are doing their job well and others to contend that they are focusing on trivia. Inspectorates have been criticised on the grounds that: they are not fair; they are not consistent; they demand too much or too little; they will put people out of business; they pursue the wrong things; they do not understand the realities of the care which they inspect; they fail to ensure a sufficient minimum.

There is a temptation to see those who criticise increased regulation as people who are out to cut corners at the expense of quality. We have to remember that some owners are people who were former managers of local authority homes and moved out in part because they wanted a greater ability to influence the quality of care. Inspection, appropriately, may require that some people improve their provision and put others out of business. On the other hand, inappropriately, inspection may force people into strait jackets and impose unnecessary demands. We have to find a neutral way to ask and answer the questions about outcome, and to determine which people should be involved in examining the activities of inspection units.

The government, which appears uncertain as to its view, having argued for moving units out of local authorities has decided that they should stay within the local authority but be subject to review by the Chief Executive of the authority (Department of Health, 1994b). The issue that is not faced is that systems and structures do not guarantee that inspectors will carry out their work in ways that others will consider sensible. Indeed, I suspect it is inevitable at times that being thought effective by one group will mean being seen as interfering by another.

The circular specified the areas on which the assessment by the Chief Executive should concentrate:

- the objectivity with which the unit applies common standards as between local authority and independent provision;
- the success of the unit in maintaining its independence within the social services department;
- the degree to which inspection reports have been made publicly available and the scope for the further

expansion of open reporting;
- the effectiveness of the social services department's follow-up where improvements in services are found to be necessary, particularly in respect of directly provided services;
- the extent to which the authority's inspection follow-up policy has been observed (Department of Health, 1994b, para. 33).

The extent to which the Chief Executive's oversight results in a useful review of the inspectorate depends on the capacity and style of individual chief executives and the processes in place in local authorities. If the fear is that Directors of Social Services might stifle impartial reporting because of their involvement in providing some of the facilities being inspected, it must be remembered that the Chief Executive, while free of the departmental responsibility, is responsible for the overall good name of the authority and has the potential to exercise even more powerful interference

Involving outsiders in inspection is another means adopted to oversee regulation. The requirements that inspectorates set up advisory panels and include lay assessors are designed with this in mind (Department of Health, 1994b). There is an important, underlying principle, that of exposing the activities of people with power to the views of others. This type of opening up is assumed to be a good thing but it is essential to work out, first, its purpose, secondly, whose version of reality or good practice is to be adopted and, thirdly, for whose benefit the process is thought to exist. The administrative implications are discussed in Chapter Seven.

In a sense the nature of the oversight of inspectorates that is thought necessary is dependent on the view that is taken of their function: are they on the side of one group or another? - users, public, politicians, local authority or even providers? The stance taken by those trying 'to guard the guards' (or control inspectorates) will differ if inspectorates are thought to be politically motivated and conducting a campaign against private providers than if they are seen as campaigners on behalf of users.

CONCLUSIONS

It is probable that the assumptions that are made about the intent of inspectorates will play a large part in the reaction to their work. This might be one of the few areas where an opinion poll in the form of an attitude survey would be useful. Indeed, it would be helpful to know what knowledge there is of inspectorates and the use that is made of them. If one measure of the activity of inspection units is the numbers of inspections which they undertake and the reports which they produce, another would be the contact made by the public: complaints, allegations, requests for advice or study of reports.

Inspectorates operate in a context of ambivalence: anxiety about the abuse that regularly is revealed in social care and concern that inspectorates may use their authority improperly. In Chapter Eight Jean Bradshaw looks at ways of assessing the effectiveness of inspectorates. Both inspectorates and their 'customers' would be helped if there was some evidence as to the quality of their work, rather than the current reliance on anecdote and assumptions about motivation. Sometimes it is hard to question what gets established as myth. The task for inspectorates is to present the case setting out the procedures which are designed to ensure that there is no favouritism. However, it is important not to gloss over the characteristics of systems or structures which could lead to differential reporting. Whether or not such differences exist will depend on the activities of the inspectorate and the steps which it takes to ensure impartiality.

Two

Being inspected: the manager's story

Jean Bradshaw and Eileen Gentry

INTRODUCTION

THIS CHAPTER focuses on some of the people subject to the inspection process: the owners, managers and staff of the services being inspected. However much they may state that they value the inspection, there are very few circumstances in which they have initiated the event. The rational self may say that the inspection is an important aspect of demonstrating to the outside world that services are safe: the reality is that inspections are likely to seem intrusive and threatening. Indeed, staff may see themselves as the 'victims' of inspection.

We draw on anecdotal evidence from a wide range of people and on literature to suggest some central themes. It is written by people who now are inspectors, but vividly remember being inspected themselves. We have tried to capture the main attitudes and issues but are aware that it is not representative of all owners and managers. Indeed, in part the material is as much the inspectorate's view of managers' perceptions. We have not carried out an attitude survey but think that we have identified some of the common responses. Indeed, a part of what we want to convey is that there is a rational response to inspections, but there is also an emotional reaction, as is argued in the Foreword and Chapter One. We may 'know' and 'think' that what we are doing is satisfactory or even good; but there lurks the fear, 'the feeling', that perhaps there are things going on that we don't know about and that we shall be caught out.

THE RANGE OF INSPECTION

One of the fundamental issues about inspection is summed up by the Social Services Inspectorate (SSI): 'being inspected is very painful; no-one likes criticism and reports always contain some criticism' (Department of Health, 1992, p.11). The Social Services Inspectorate concentrated in that report on inspection of local authority services but the impact of criticism is no different for those in the independent sector.

The impact of inspection raises a welter of feelings in different people, from fear, anxiety, anger, concern and irritation to pleasure, gratitude, relief or pride. The negative feelings seem to be more prevalent than the positive ones and this may well relate to two factors highlighted by the Social Services Inspectorate. It contends, first, that 'inspections are seen as 'catching out' exercises rather than as a means of promoting the quality of care for clients' and, secondly, that 'inspection reports did not acknowledge the good practices that managers knew existed' (Department of Health, 1992, pp.13 & 16).

Some of the feelings and issues raised by being inspected are the same for people in different types of residential homes. However, in order to explore the subject further we have divided our material into four groups: residential homes for adults in the independent sector, local authority managed residential homes for adults, children's services (residential homes, schools and day care) and lastly special inspections or investigations. It should be noted that we use the phrase residential homes for adults to encompass all types of residential homes for adults: people with physical or learning disabilities, people with alcohol or drug related problems, people with mental illness, older people. The themes which emerge in the discussion of one sector may well be significant to the others. The different requirements made of different types of facility (local authority/independent, children/adult, residential/day) are discussed more fully in later chapters. What matters here is that there are distinctions, in particular that since local authority establishments do not have to register their facilities, they cannot be refused permission to open by the inspectorate and cannot be faced with moves to take away registration. In the documents setting out guidance for inspectors, there are also substantial differences for adult and children's services in terms of style, focus and detail.

ADULT SERVICES IN THE INDEPENDENT SECTOR

The following account is developed from the personal experience of an independent sector manager:

> It was two years after registration that we had our first inspection. We had had an inspector pop in once but she only stayed for a few minutes and there was no feedback. The new inspector had been known to me when he was a manager of a residential home. I had regularly visited 'his home' in the past, supervising students. It had recently closed because of the new requirements on inspecting local authority homes. The letter announcing the inspection visit brought a mixed response from the staff: 'We'll show him how a residential establishment should be run!' from some; 'Who does he think he is?' from others; while a third group said 'This will be a good opportunity to have an objective view of how we are doing'.
>
> The temperature increased on a pre-inspection visit. We had been totally unaware of the powers an inspector had. We had worked very hard to promote ownership

and privacy for residents and it seemed that a man whom no-one knew could cut right across this. I think the shock was equal on his side! After a long debate we agreed some compromises: first, he would view files only with the resident present; and, secondly, he would not enter bedrooms if the person was not present and invited him in, unless he had any reason to be concerned about the welfare of the resident or suspicious of the reason why people did not want him to go in.

The 'residential home' could perhaps be best described as one of several flats in a main block, with other houses adjacent. Several of the residents had been described as 'challenging' in the past. Indeed, some of the staff were challenging too – but that was part of their training. The inspector continued to be accommodating and accepted an invitation to the next staff meeting. This did little to reduce the hostility of staff who were loyal to the people living in the scheme, their staff colleagues and the manager/proprietor. It is worth noting that the language of the inspection was itself difficult: although we were registered as a 'residential home', we did not talk about the place as a 'home' nor did we refer to the people who lived there as 'residents'.

I wrote to everyone living in the scheme explaining what the inspector was there for and what he could do. Most could not read, but the letter at least indicated that there was an important point for discussion. It provided a reason to explain individually to each person what the inspection was about. The staff team as a whole emphasised that the focus of the inspection was the staff and the 'home', with the aim of protecting the 'residents'. Nevertheless, our approach had the opposite of the intended effect: some residents were outraged; others suspicious, wondering whether we had done something wrong.

Things got worse. For reasons that were not

explained to us, the chief inspector was to be involved in the inspection as well. Probably this was more daunting to the inspector than to us, as we knew the chief inspector did not have experience of residential work. This highlighted the main focus of hostility: we were being inspected by a department which provided no residential care for the user group with whom we were working, which provided no funding for our scheme and which had an inspectorate made up of people who largely did not have a background in residential work! We thought that we, the staff and residents, were in a better position to judge the quality of what we were doing than they were.

The day of the inspection arrived. I had dressed up for it, of course. My shiny image did not last for long. Someone managed to prise the washing matching open while it was operating and, as I dealt with a screaming woman and a flood, my smart gear was reduced to a soggy mess. Luckily I kept painting trousers in the building; less impressive, no doubt – but much more in keeping with normal life in the establishment.

I had insisted that time be made for each person to meet the inspector and talk in private if he or she wished. Even the most belligerent wanted this opportunity. The inspector stuck to the rules about files, though we managed to use this slightly to our advantage simply by making sure certain people were around at the right time. Some people are better at keeping files than others and we considered much of the information to be private and not simply confidential. (Perhaps inspectors are right to be suspicious!)

In the end, the only sticking point seemed to be administration. It wasn't that we didn't have what he wanted – we didn't have it *how* he wanted it! He suggested that the system might work for us but wondered whether someone else could step in and cope. 'Come the nuclear holocaust', we thought, 'will anyone else be able to take over!' Other than this, there was little feedback. We could only assume other things were all right.

The report took two months to come. It was an anxious time. There was an awareness that we could call the inspector's bluff. The social services department could not afford to lose our scheme, which was thought to be well run and, certainly, appeared to be very well respected locally. What could the inspector make us do? At the same time it was like waiting for the results of an exam, and one in which you felt *they* could make up what should have been in the answers.

When the report arrived it was read and discussed by staff and manager. We were not happy. Users had been identified, if not by name then by descriptions of their behaviour. Terms were used which we had worked hard to lose: 'attention seeking' and 'mental handicap', for example. We wrote a lengthy response. I have it on good authority that the inspector was stunned by this.

To his credit yet again, he visited and after lengthy discussion we agreed on amendments.

The staff were still unhappy that there was very little on the positive aspects of the scheme while the criticisms remained, amended as they had been. It had been explained prior to the visit that we could only be 'satisfactory' – this was their highest accolade.

The surprising part of this tale is that we developed a worthwhile relationship with the inspector. It seemed to us that he had a genuine respect for the scheme and the people and staff in it. We took note of the recommendations if only to ensure that he would have nothing to criticise next time. He didn't.

Some may read this and feel it is unrepresentative. What about the possibility of a devious manager with a badly run home? Yes, we could have covered up some things. The dilemma that underlies inspection is whether it is easy or difficult to get beneath the surface of life in the facility being inspected. At times those being inspected, the inspectees, feel that their whole lives are being revealed with every gesture open to interpretation. At others, they are aware of the way in which inspectors can be 'guided' and 'led', if not influenced. Inspectors will have the same mix of views: they may think their thorough inspection, with opportunities for users to comment, will leave no stone unturned or they may be conscious of the limitations of their knowledge. Certainly more will be known (and less can be hidden) if there is preparation for the inspection and if inspections take place outside office hours.

Of course, managers do not know the significance of the inspection report for users or social service department purchasers. Will people use it to choose between homes? Reports which to the manager appear pernickety could make all the difference to where a prospective resident decides to go, whether or not she/he directly reads the report. Few homes are in the charmed position of having a guaranteed demand and a substantial waiting list. In a competitive business, few proprietors will call the inspector's bluff.

It may be argued that quality assurance, being a system by which the organisation assumes responsibility for the assuring of its own performance, is more important than inspection. Might it be that a British Standard inspectorate will not need to inspect a British Standard home! Perhaps it will be quality assurance rather than inspection which will drive up standards above the minimum, which is seldom adequate for everyone. At the inspection of our home, it would have been nice to have had advice and not just criticism. Indeed, we would have wanted our internal quality assurance measures to be have been considered by inspectors, especially as they might have been more enlightening than brief chats with people.

Most managers by now are pretty good at performing for inspectors. Most inspectors are pretty good at scratching the veneer. In many parts of the country it has taken some time for a *modus vivendi* to be worked out between inspectors and managers which includes agreement about the inspection agenda and the process. Hopefully, both managers and inspectors will have the same aims of wanting to improve services, of involving service users and never being content with 'good enough'. There needs to be open discussion about the route to achieve this. It may seem like a game of outwitting the inspector or catching out the manager/ proprietor, but it is one with a deadly serious side, the focus of which is the life of a resident.

As managers, we want to be understood. We want our problems to be recognised, our skills recorded and we want our achievements catalogued. Tempting as it is to put the whole blame for what goes wrong during inspections on the inspector, and the total credit when things go well on the manager, obviously, there is responsibility on both parties for events. In fact there is a negotiation between inspector and manager, even though it may not be termed that. Certainly there is truth in the notion that managers can manage (or rather 'influence') the inspection. Perhaps there should be courses in 'The management of inspectors'!

When relationships between the two parties are good and the manager has confidence in the work of the inspector, we may be lulled into a false sense of security. In what sense can inspections ever be 'partnerships'? Where does the power lie? Are inspectors at their most dangerous when they are pleasant?

From the perspective of the independent sector owner or manager it is hard to work out the relationships between inspectorate, the person purchasing the care and the individual home as provider. In the world of purchasers and providers the relationships between them, and their individual relationships with the inspectorates are immensely important. The purchaser may be the prospective resident or a relative negotiating on her/his behalf; increasingly, the purchaser is likely to be a professional: assessor, care manager or social worker. Certainly, independent sector managers know only too well that the purchaser has to be convinced of the quality of their product. We wrote earlier of the feeling of waiting for exam results.

This dimension adds a new set of anxieties as there is another set of ground rules to work out: it may be that there are two examiners, working to different curricula and different methods of assessment.

LOCAL AUTHORITY PROVIDERS OF RESIDENTIAL HOMES FOR ADULTS

Some of the issues raised in the case study above apply equally to local authority providers but some things are different. Drawing on the Social Services Inspectorate Report and personal experiences the main focus of this section will be on the differences between the sectors. The report states: 'The location of Inspection Units in Social Services Departments means that inevitably there will be tensions' (Department of Health, 1992, p.7).

One of the feelings of the manager within the independent sector home, mentioned at the start of this chapter, was betrayal: 'Surely, he of all people should have understood us!'. The inspection unit staff may be viewed by staff from local authority homes as 'one of us' or 'the enemy within'. These two ends of the spectrum bring the separate dangers of collusion or feelings of betrayal.

Add to this the fact that many inspectors and local authority provider staff had been colleagues immediately prior to the development of the 'arms length' inspectorate and no wonder there are tensions. Each side knows each other's credentials, qualities and shortcomings. People on both 'sides' were heard saying 'I knew him/her when s/he was only a ...' and 'What right has s/he to judge me!'

Before the start of the 'arms length' inspection process in local authority residential homes, a range of feelings was expressed:

> - s/he does not know the first thing about running a home so s/he better not pretend otherwise;
>
> they know the problems in the department, so they will make allowances;

it will be good to be judged alongside the private sector, we know our buildings may not be as good but our care standards are better;

it will be useful to have an outsider's view of this home to help me improve practice here;

this is a good home and I don't want any nonsense from these jumped up inspectors;

this is a waste of time; I know what is wrong here but I do not have the resources to change it.

Given this range of feelings, the preparation given to local authority provider staff before inspections started too often was very limited. Many had no knowledge of the Registered Homes Act, 1984, nor, more importantly, of the accompanying Regulations. Thus, they had no idea of what was required of them. Some of those who were aware of the requirements thought that many of them were irrelevant and applied only to the independent sector. Others were also unclear about the process, the rights of the inspectors and the standards against which they were being inspected. Whose job it was to do this preparation was never established, so no wonder tensions arose.

The impact of the first inspection in most homes was marked. In some cases this was caused by the process and in others by the outcome, that is the report. Some of the issues raised by the process were:

- bewilderment and confusion because no one knew what was expected;
- fear and anxiety as people felt under scrutiny and subject to personal criticism;
- anger about the intrusiveness of the process or the preoccupation with detailed administrative procedures;
- relief that it had gone smoothly;
- disappointment that the important issues had been ignored;
- pleasure at finding another channel to try and get things improved.

Then the reports arrived. Many people found these a surprise. Was this a consequence of the inspectors finding it difficult to share their findings at the time of the inspection because of previous colleague relationships? Was it because managers did not expect shortcomings to be recorded? Was it a question of settling old scores? Or was it that what is said seems harsher when written down? The anecdotal evidence of much anger being generated following the receipt of these first reports is endorsed by the SSI. When managers received the reports from inspectors, some acted on the assumption that they did not have to do anything about the requirements. The confusion was compounded by uncertainty as to who had the responsibility for taking action, the head of the unit or the outside line manager. The way in which this has been handled has dictated the outcome of future relationships.

As a consequence of those first contacts, there are homes where inspectors will always be feared and others where they will always be dismissed as irrelevant but, in most, accommodation has been made on both sides. Important issues have been addressed by local authority providers about such issues as health and safety but there remains a concern that inspection is about the bureaucracy, not the care.

In the three years which have passed since inspections of local authority homes for adults commenced, has anything changed? Inevitably it has: in most cases working relationships have been established, inspectors are tolerated or even welcomed. Some of this comes down to personalities and individual relationships. The responses to inspection of local authority providers capture the ambivalence to inspection. On the one hand it is viewed as an irritant that gets in the way of the real work, a game in which a good report can be achieved if the recommendations in the last report are implemented; on the other, it is seen as something demanding careful preparation so that problems are hidden. Yet others may see inspection as another method of putting the case for improvements or a genuine opportunity to have the work reviewed by someone from outside the home.

There is still a major tension as to whether an inspection unit may be truly independent if it is part of a social services department, an issue that was raised in Chapter One. This causes concern for the independent sector but there are issues for local authority managers too. Some feel the inspectorate has no real teeth: it may raise issues in successive inspection reports but nothing will change as decisions will be made elsewhere. Alternatively, managers feel that some inspectors bend over backwards to prove that they do not favour local authority homes and so are hypercritical of the local authority homes. A recent comment made when discussing the need for equivalence between the independent sector and the local authority was: 'I do not understand the need for it, the local authority can regulate its own establishments without inspectors, it is the private sector that needs to be checked up on.' Indeed, any organisation may think that it is able to regulate its own provision: it is others which need inspection to keep them up to the mark. The issue is wider than the location of the inspectorates inside or outside social services departments: at its heart is the question whether regulation is really thought to be necessary or whether it is regarded as a cosmetic exercise.

CHILDREN'S SERVICES

Inspection of children's services by local authority inspectorates started later and has operated only since the Children Act came into force in October 1991. In this area inspection was scheduled to begin in the independent sector and the local authority at the same time, although once again there are differences in relation to the registration of facilities in each sector. As in the rest of this chapter, this section is based on views and opinions made to inspectors and may not be representative.

Many of the reactions to being inspected have mirrored those in the adult residential sector but there are some differences. The first of these relates to inspections of independent boarding schools. Most head teachers and proprietors of these schools could see no necessity for inspection at all. After all, their establishments often were well known, many of them being famous public schools at which the country's leaders had been educated. Moreover, parents chose to send their children there and that choice within the marketplace should provide a sufficient guarantee of quality. In one authority a principal inspector commented:

> The prevalent view among the schools is that parents are the most effective scrutinisers ... It was thought that because parents bought this education, they were largely its inspectors (Kingston P., 1994).

To add insult to injury these inspections were to be conducted by social services departments. What would their inspectors understand of education and, in particular, of residential education? Might they be antagonistic to the very notion of boarding schools and out to put their political prejudice into effect? Indeed, might they be 'woolly, wet, lefty social workers'? What did they know about anything and what right did they have to comment on the highly professional practice of well qualified teaching staff?

> Introducing inspectors to private boarding schools brought together two groups foreign to each other's ways, he said (Dr Hearnden, general secretary of the Independent Schools Joint Council [ISJC]). On some schools' part there was the suspicion that they faced people ideologically opposed to private education. Some inspectors, on the other hand, detected from schools an attitude that they were intruding into areas which they did not understand, even in some cases that the schools considered themselves above the process of inspection.
>
> 'Social services' main concern is with children in children's homes...They have never really been concerned professionally with mainstream education (Kingston P., 1994).

The second issue that was different was in relation to day care services for under 8s. There was a feeling that all these rules and regulations would stop people running much needed services for young children. Providers felt unable to meet the standards and thought they would either stop operating or would have to put their charges up to make the improvements. Similar points were made by providers of residential homes and schools in the independent and local authority sectors.

As with the adult sector, inspectors might be criticised either for not having the appropriate expertise to understand the task of those whom they were inspecting or for not understanding the demands and complexities of running a business. It was all very well for these local government officers to have these high aspirations about good child care practice but they were sheltered from the hard financial realities. Let them try to do all that at an economic cost!

Despite these problems, many managers and proprietors welcomed the inspectors advice and wanted to achieve high quality standards. One local authority inspectorate reported that 'Schools had gone to considerable lengths and expense...to implement suggestions', while a schools' representative said that 'the initial wave of inspections had been very helpful', particularly with reference to child protection procedures (Kingston, 1994). However, the ISJC has lobbied the Government, it would appear with success, to have inspections take place much less frequently at four yearly intervals. Schools have also been aware, as have managers of other establishments, that in a competitive market, inspection reports might have more impact on their business than was initially appreciated.

A recent research study conducted in Cumbria has demonstrated that the pupils in the schools inspected value the involvement of the inspectors and would welcome more frequent unannounced visits (see Chapter Five). In addition, written and verbal appreciation has been received from heads of schools following inspections. The Draft Guidance (Department of Health, 1994d) recently issued for consultation identifies circumstances in which less frequent inspections could be undertaken. Given these guidelines, the extent to which there will be fewer inspections is open to question. In Cumbria only 1 out of 16 schools meets the criteria for reduced inspection and the head of this school has said that more frequent visits by inspectors would be welcomed. All of this seems to indicate a more positive view of regulation since the establishment of the inspection process.

SPECIAL INSPECTIONS AND INVESTIGATIONS

This section has been compiled from personal experience and from interviewing staff from adult residential homes and child care settings where special investigations or inspections have occurred. All of these investigations took place as a result of the death of a service user in unusual and tragic circumstances, so all the staff involved in these special inspections were coping with a traumatic situation. Many were facing personal loss and grief over the death as well as supporting the bereaved relatives. Guilt is a normal reaction to any death but particularly one that is accidental and has occurred in tragic circumstances. In these situations this guilt was compounded by someone investigating or inspecting to see what had gone wrong.

In all these situations, the way the inspection/investigation was handled and how people were treated was of vital importance. Most of the people interviewed thought they were treated with respect and concern, this making it easier for them to answer any questions. There was one situation in which one inspector was perceived by several members of staff to be insensitive and to adopt an inquisitorial style, described from the perspective of the interviewee as 'being subjected to the third degree'. The anger about this was still apparent over two years later. Even in situations where this extreme style was not thought to have been used, some care assistants found the language used by interviewers hard to understand and thought that terms were not explained to them. They realised later, when they received written notes of the interviews, that this communication problem was two way, and their answers had not been understood by the interviewers. It is possible also that the interviewees may not have said either what they intended or what, at a later time, they wished.

Most people realised why the investigation or inspection was necessary but, at the same time, resented the intrusion at such a sensitive time. Some were very open and felt they had nothing to hide and the investigation/inspection would only show that there was no one to blame and the standard of practice was good. Other people were extremely angry, citing their own good track record and the fact that serious incidents elsewhere had not always been subjected to this process; they thought the whole event was a personal affront to their professional integrity. This was compounded by the feeling of being invaded and taken over at a time when people needed privacy and an opportunity to gain comfort and support from those whom they trusted and with whom they worked.

For the managers who were not 'hands on', that is the line managers outside the home, the feelings were different: dread and panic might be the first reaction to the investigation/inspection. This was followed by a need to organise things for the inspectors and check that everything, such as files, was in order; this was described by one person as 'the hygiene issues'. Then there was the manager's anxiety for the staff being inspected and ensuring support for them, but all the time there was the nagging doubt about what would be discovered. 'What more should I have done?'

In a number of these inspections, people had been interviewed three times as there was a police investigation, a management investigation and an inspection. Some people thought this was unnecessary but others could see that the three investigations had different purposes. Some even found it therapeutic to go over the events a number of times.

The method of recording interviews varied but where notes were taken by a secretary or an inspector, the people interviewed universally were dissatisfied with the result and thought it did not represent what they had said. In most circumstances tape recorders had not been used as it was thought these would intimidate people and would create more material than could be processed. However, in the situations where interviews were taped, every individual was asked in advance and no one refused; the only person who had any reservations was a senior manager who had worked as an inspector. Some taped interviews were typed verbatim and others were summarised but in either case interviewees felt reasonably satisfied with what was recorded, which was not the case in situations where notes were taken. In nearly all of these special investigations/ inspections those interviewed did see a transcript of their own interview and have an opportunity to comment prior to it being finalised and this process was much appreciated especially in the situations where people thought the first report was very inaccurate. Some of the interviewees' requests for alterations were accepted but some were not and in a few cases this caused concern, particularly where this was thought to have been due to a communication problem. In all cases where people remained dissatisfied they could append their version of the event.

The focus of the inspection/investigation was rarely mentioned by those interviewed, but there were similar questions raised to those in previous sections of this chapter about the inspectors' knowledge or experience in the relevant field. One person interviewed thought that inspectors were looking for the ideal when they should have made their assessment against a 'good enough' standard. There was also some frustration about inspectors identifying things which, as a consequence of their report, were put right after the tragedy; when staff and managers had raised these same issues earlier, nothing had been done. One manager said, 'It is sickening the things which are put right afterwards that you could not get done before'.

The reactions of staff and managers to the reports varied according to the contents and the perception of the situation.

Two members of staff reacted to the same report in very different ways. One thought the report was very unfair and did not give a true picture and that it was very unjust to the manager. The other was relieved that problems had been identified and were out in the open; she had felt unable to voice her concerns before as she believed that anyone who criticised the situation was victimised. Even where reports were largely positive, it was noticeable that everyone homed in on the negative comments, particularly if they perceived criticism levelled at themselves. In one situation the staff and managers who had been subjected to the investigation never saw the report and the verbal feedback given was judged unhelpful. The manager in this situation felt she was left to resolve problems that had been identified but she was unclear about exactly what the problems were or the standards expected of her and the staff.

One long term effect on all these staff groups was a feeling of stigmatisation. They considered that they had been stigmatised by the initial tragedy and this was then compounded by the investigation/inspection. If the report was positive some people thought this helped their public image but others felt the 'no smoke without fire' principle was dominant.

CONCLUSION

Some themes have emerged that will be explored in other chapters. We have drawn largely on the perceptions of one group of people on the receiving end of inspection: the owners and managers. These views raise important issues:

- the credibility and professionalism of the inspectors;
- the value of good preparation and planning;
- the balance between consistency and flexibility;
- the need to emphasise the positives as well as being appropriately critical;
- the power of the inspector;
- the meaning of 'being at arms length';
- the use of language;

- how judgements are made;
- the viability of the systems for ensuring quality.

The themes are integral to later chapters but we must remind ourselves that owners and managers have different interests to inspectors. Inspectors should not have the satisfaction of this group of 'customers' as their main aim; their task is to regulate, which may not be compatible with everybody expressing satisfaction.

Three

Listening to the views of the service user

Albert Cook and Eileen Gentry

INTRODUCTION

THE PAST decade has witnessed a major shift in attempts to bring about change in the relationship between those who provide services and those who receive them.

The Registered Homes Act 1984, corresponding Regulations (1984) and subsequent amendments (1991), have sought to control the operation of residential homes and nursing homes in order that those receiving care are safeguarded. The Children Act (1989), with its Notes of Guidance, similarly has emphasised the regulation of residential schools, children's homes and day care for children under eight. The emphasis of the Registered Homes Act is on the duty of the person operating the service to provide care and welfare for the resident and, perhaps as a secondary consideration, to 'so far as is practicable, ascertain the wishes and feelings of the resident and give due regard to them as is reasonable given the resident's age and understanding' (Regulation 9).

The introduction of inspection units into the world of residential and day care has been accompanied by government initiatives to promote quality and empower the user. The Citizen's Charter, the Patient's Charter, the Parent's Charter and Charter Marks are all claimed as attempts to balance the relationship between the provider and the recipient of the service.

The Citizen's Charter suggested that the central purpose of inspection in social and other services is 'to check that the professional services that the public receive are delivered in the most effective way possible and genuinely meet the needs of those whom they serve'. The public concerns to which inspectorates must be responsive start with concerns and wishes of service users. It is essential therefore, in the Government's view, that inspectorate's combine their professional knowledge, expertise and standards with the views and insights of members of the wider public and that both the registration and inspection process are open and accessible (Department of Health, 1994b, para.1).

The disability rights movement and the concept of ordinary living have also been significant influences focusing attention on the importance of the service user's role.

Given the significant, indeed unique, position of service users as recipients of the service, it is surprising that greater attention has not been focused upon their views. In this chapter we explore the valuable contribution that can be made by those who receive the service to the success of the inspection process. We discuss the prevailing ethos in residential care, current practice, and the barriers to obtaining residents' views. Various methods and approaches are considered which allow users' views to be better incorporated into the process of inspection.

THE PREVAILING ETHOS IN RESIDENTIAL CARE

Adults and children moving to a residential home may come from:

1. their own homes or those of relatives; in a sense from an 'ordinary' domestic setting;
2. a hospital where they have lived for a long time;
3. a hospital where they have been for only a short time as a result of an acute episode or short term treatment of a chronic condition;
4. another type of residential establishment, for example from a larger home to what is called a group home;
5. a foster home, where arrangements have broken down.

The experience differs dependent both on the place from where the person has come and the nature of the reason for the move. Some may expect this to be their home for life or indeed their final home. There are residents who never come to terms with the trauma of the change and the new experience, and this may not be because they are not well cared for but because it is not their own home and because they are devastated by the events that have led to their move. An Inspector once asked a resident , 'Are you happy here?'. With a wry smile the reply came back, 'How can you be happy anywhere but in a home of your own? But the staff do their best to make life comfortable for me'.

However much statements of principle emphasise, as does the Wagner Report (1988) that residential life is to be a positive experience, for many at best it is the least bad alternative and not the stuff of dreams. There are some situations when the life style has been chosen, if not by the individual users themselves, then by their relatives and is regarded positively by the people who live in the establishment. This may be how a move to a residential home is perceived by some adults; more typically, it is the position of children in day care and young people in residential schools regarded as 'ordinary boarding schools' rather than 'special schools'.

The implementation of 'Community Care' has increased the pace at which people with learning disabilities and mental health problems have moved (or been moved) from hospital to 'the community'. The long term effects of life in hospitals, with its tendency to institutionalise, and the ways people adapted (by learning particular survival skills, which might be adaptive or maladaptive, for example learned helplessness) are well documented. (See Clough, 1981, p.8 and 1982 for a summary of the literature.) The shift from hospital life to what is described as an environment of choice and individual decision making is not easy.

Those who have carried out inspections of services, as other visitors, often will have observed the imbalance of power between resident and member of staff. This is hardly surprising when one considers that a resident is dependent upon others for many aspects of their daily living. In such circumstances residents tend to think that they must show gratitude to staff and are unlikely to question or complain about the service they receive. There is recognition of this in the literature: Clough, (1981, pp.151-165) discusses power, dependency and gratitude; Ward (1993, pp.9-14) writes about power, prejudice and dependency as three key issues in residential life.

People who receive residential care services often find themselves within a regime which will be unlike any other situation in their life's experience. To share one's life with others who are unrelated, to fit into the demands and needs of other people, to require the assistance of others before one is able to carry out the tasks of daily living are all facets of a lifestyle unknown to people who have enjoyed the independence of living life in their own home.

BARRIERS TO OBTAINING RESIDENTS' VIEWS

The inspector, in carrying out an inspection of the service, will have to overcome a number of factors which limit the likelihood of service users telling inspectors what they think of the facility: the conflict of loyalties for residents who want to support staff as well as express dissatisfaction; as discussed earlier, the nature of dependency and power, and the expectations of resident gratitude; staff who may inhibit the residents' ability to complain; institutional practice, which does not encourage suggestions or improvements to the life in the home; the difficulties in communicating with the resident because of speech or language difficulties.

New residents will be confronted with a strange situation, having to adapt to a new lifestyle with little idea of what to expect or of what comprises quality of service because they have never lived in a residential home before.

Care managers, in implementing the NHS and Community Care Act 1990, are expected to pursue a policy where the choice of users and carers is to be regarded as of major importance. In practice, however, there are often constraining factors which limit the realisation of the resident's choice. Relatives may play a dominant part in decisions, for example selecting a home which provides easy access for them rather than maintains the past links of the older person. Alternatively, choice may be limited by or dependent upon where vacancies exist. One of the consequences is that it may not be easy to move from a place about which one may wish to complain.

THE INSPECTION PROCESS

In the course of a visit to an establishment the inspector will use observation skills, inspect records, and talk to management, staff and users. For childminding, this will probably take place on one occasion per year; for other day and residential centres there are likely to two or three inspection visits in a year. As we have seen in Chapter Two some heads of residential schools have argued that this should be reduced substantially and the same has been argued by some owners of residential homes.

The early development of registration and inspection focused on compliance to Regulations through the checking of records and the physical standard of the home. Both aspects are important. As a consequence a considerable part of the inspection has been spent on discussions with the owner or manager in the office, on observing physical standards in the building and on checking records. Most inspectors would wish to see a more balanced approach to the inspection where far more time is allocated to obtaining the views of service users.

The emphasis on the achievement of hard data to demonstrate the effectiveness of the inspection process gradually is being supported by the views of residents on what life is like.

Whatever the frequency of inspections, and whatever is determined as the focus, the inspector has to decide how to get the required information. In particular, on the theme of this chapter, the crux is the amount of time to be spent with service users (including their carers) and the methods to be used to find their perspective. The time available for inspection is limited; nevertheless, within that limited time, inspectorate staff have to work out the priority which they give to users' views: how valuable is the time spent with the service user? how essential is the user's perspective to an understanding of how a place operates and to a successful outcome for the inspection? There are some who would even go so far as to say that inspection of a service should be seen through the eyes of the service user.

Those familiar with the inspection process will know the bad practice which can exist: the inspector visits and spends several hours in conference with the manager of the home; users are aware of the visit as the office becomes out of bounds for the duration; just as most are settling down to a short siesta after lunch, the inspector descends on the lounge, sits down and states to no-one in particular whom he/she is and the purpose of the visit; if the opportunity is created to speak to an individual in private ('Show me your room!') then this conversation may focus on a range of topics from meals to sex !

Most inspectors are dissatisfied with this, and acknowledge the difficulties of wanting to talk with residents without imposing on them. However, there are few documented accounts of more imaginative practice. The will to get users' views may be there but the process still be ineffective.

OBTAINING THE VIEWS OF RESIDENTS

Gathering information

Inspectors will gain some picture of care practice and what is offered to the resident through studying records, brochures and contracts. This material cannot give information as to how each person perceives what life is like in the home for her or himself. Staff cannot provide that perspective because their perception of life in the home will be different to that of residents.

Inspection is a snapshot of life which should include the experience of users. Consulting with users:

1. provides the inspector with first hand knowledge of care and quality of life in the home;
2. makes an explicit, public statement about the value of each person's view; *and*
3. fulfils the purpose of informing users of the range and quality of services in their own home and to some extent in others. A strong case can be made for ensuring that the views of users form an integral part of any inspection. Decisions have to be taken about the process: what sort of information? how is it to be collected?

Preparation for obtaining the views of the resident during inspection

Obtaining residents' views requires preparation with them as part of the inspection process. To gain useful information from residents will require careful planning to gain their confidence and trust. A simple courtesy is an introductory letter from the inspector, with a photograph and some brief information. Establishing trust is a two way process.

The assistance of the manager will need to be sought to establish effective communication with residents. Correspondence with the manager should not only include information on the inspection process but also on the need to discuss inspection with the residents. An agreement needs to be reached between inspectorate and manager as to the responsibility which falls on each of them related to the preparation of residents for the inspection. From the manager's perspective discussion of a forthcoming inspection is part of wider discussions with residents, whether individually or in small groups; it should include details on the rights of inspectors and the rights of residents in the inspection process. Too often managers who do attempt to do this raise anxieties about matters such as access to files without discussing the core components of inspection: the legal requirements, the aspects of safeguarding the residents and examination of the service. Inspectors will be well aware of managers who project their own perceptions of rights and privacy through the residents rather than providing balanced information which can then be brought to the attention of the inspector as part of the preparation process.

Inspectorates may wish also to communicate directly with residents. They should provide straightforward information to residents on the standards that they are looking for and which should be offered in residential care homes so that residents are able to form a judgement about the standards which exist in the home where they live. The format of the information must be appropriate to the people for whom it is intended: clearly written brochures, with availability in languages other than English: large print versions; tape recordings. As the residents usually only have experience of one residential home, the inspector may help to raise awareness of standards existing in other homes.

An introductory meeting between residents and the inspector can be used to clarify and discuss issues and information relating to the inspection process. This visit should be timetabled to fit with the normal pattern of activities in the home and will often be an evening visit. It may be left to the inspector to raise issues about privacy and confidentiality. How many residents know they have a file, never mind whether they are concerned about the inspector looking at it ?

In some homes residents will have advocates, either to facilitate group meetings or to represent a particular individual in the home. They too should be present at this introductory visit. It is vital that the process of inspection is kept in the minds of residents rather than be a once or twice a year event and advocates can help to facilitate this.

Confidentiality

One topic that should be included in the preparation for the inspection, perhaps in a written brochure as well as in discussion, is that of the use to which the information will be put. The inspector has to determine the limits to free information, privacy and confidentiality. Typically, inspectors talk with users rather than conduct more formal interviews. This means that the inspector has to decide, given the time available, the extent to which the conversation must be focused and the extent to which it is reasonable for the inspector to listen to whatever the user wants to discuss. There also has to be clarity as to the parts of information that may be stored and used for reporting on the inspection and the parts that will remain confidential to inspector and user. It is difficult, indeed dangerous, to guarantee confidentiality before knowing the nature of the information. Inspectors may be given information which they must not keep confidential, perhaps because it affects the safety and welfare of others who live in the establishment.

There are some aspects of the information that an inspector has no need to report to staff or to use in a report, for example that two people have a fulfilling, sexual relationship; it is not the responsibility of the inspector to inform staff that this is occurring. It is helpful for the inspector to test such information against the purpose of an inspection which is to find out abut care practices, the establishment and its environment. It is these, not the resident, which is the subject of the inspection. However, the difficulty for the inspector in guaranteeing confidentiality in advance of hearing what is said is that some aspect of what is a private matter may be germane to the understanding of the quality of life.

The dilemma of sorting priorities between protection of the resident, the confidential nature of the information which may be given to a 'stranger' and the need to safeguard those in residential care is a continuing one for the inspector. These ethical dilemmas should be constantly re-examined within registration and inspection units and a clear philosophy established on dealing with information.

GETTING THE VIEWS OF THE RESIDENTS

The process of inspection can also be determined at a preparatory meeting. The requirements of legislation will continue to dictate that much of the focus is on administration, the purpose of the meeting with residents will be to emphasise that the central task for the inspector is to ascertain, with the help of residents, what the quality of life is like in the home. At this stage agreement will have to be reached with residents as to the way in which they will be involved in the inspection process, including the parameters so far as residents are concerned and the methods for collecting their views. Residents' opinions should be sought on whether they wish to be involved in viewing and explaining the contents of personal records and on whether there are intimate details which they would prefer not to be seen by inspectors and which they contend do not directly reflect on care planning or the inspection process.

Some people will want discussion in private, others with a representative or in a small group; in some homes for people with disabilities, residents might be involved in practically the whole inspection visit. People's different opinions should all be accommodated if possible, which often will mean arranging a separate visit to residents as well as that on the day of inspection.

Inspectors have to consider the implications of different ways of collecting information. Whatever the format, the key issue related to any method of collecting information emerges: the information sought must be related to an objective and a purpose. Inspectors should be asking why they want that particular information and to what use they will put it.

Questionnaires

The way in which questions are put influences the responses. The type of question is an important first issue. The questions in questionnaires will have been worked out in advance. This should mean that there has been thought about the key areas on which information is required and to the questions which will lead to the appropriate information. The questions may be of different types: ticking boxes, choice between 'Yes/ No' responses, requests for lists of factors, for example those that are liked or disliked, or opportunities to write at greater length about aspects of life in the home. The difficulties with questionnaires are those that are familiar to anyone who has conducted research: the potential for poor response rates; inappropriately completed questionnaires; the way some people are put off by them, while others are unable to complete them; the mass of information that may be too great to process in a way that justifies the amount of time given by the respondents. Their advantages are their specificity, the saving in time from conducting interviews and the fact that they can be completed anonymously. Advocates could be used to help residents complete questionnaires in situations where that is thought beneficial by the resident.

Open discussion

On the other hand material gathered by open discussion may be wide ranging and, for the purposes of inspection, irrelevant. Just because we often can glean interesting information about an individual or others within the home, this does not always mean that we should. The temptation is to amass any quantity of information in the hope that this will be part of the development of communication and may inadvertently bring forth the information sought for the purposes of inspection. The casual chat between a resident and an inspector may or may not be useful in terms of information pertinent to the inspection, and may or may not be effective in terms of inspector's time. As we have noted, it has dangers of being intrusive.

Open and closed questions

Talking with residents (whether called interviewing, talking or chatting) will require structuring but a crucial skill is that of flexibility. One dimension to consider is the advantages and disadvantages of open and closed questions. Open questions such as 'Tell me about your day' may start a conversation with some residents and bring forth wide ranging information. The question will also silence many people and leave them searching for the 'right answer'. Closed questions need not necessarily limit the range of information obtained provided the inspector is responsive. Representatives or advocates of residents may need guidance to ensure the resident's view is forthcoming as distinct from the advocate's view - which may be of equal significance.

Feeling and being free to talk

The role of grateful resident will be familiar to the inspector. The inspector also has to be aware that there are pressures on residents to comply with the regimes of the home. Residents may be served food which they find distasteful but will often say, 'I only ate a little as I wasn't hungry'. The most assertive of us can fall into the role of being compliant. We may recall a stay in hospital where we so easily become 'patients'. Going with the resident to a different place in the home, walking with in the garden or talking to them in a different setting altogether may encourage someone to see herself/himself as a person with high self esteem and much higher expectations. Evidence from investigations in children's homes is that residents may be able or willing to put forward their perception of events only when being interviewed away from the premises .

It is not easy to find or use alternative venues. Homes have a duty of care and may be reluctant to 'allow' residents to leave the premises with the inspector. There may be practical difficulties relating to the care needed by the resident. Dropping in on the range of places that some residents visit can be useful. Many people will attend day centres, adult training centres, social education centres, clubs, or colleges.

While there, the 'resident' may become someone with hopes and aspirations that may allow for more objective reflection on life in the home.

Differing perceptions of residents and staff on quality of life

A range of questionnaires on quality of life and residents' views are available. Increasingly managers are using these as internal quality assurance measures; however consideration is needed of whether the information received, in effect the outcome of such questionnaires, represents the resident's view. Certainly questionnaires cannot substitute for, though may complement, the one to one conversation between inspector and resident.

In a project using Ager's (1990) life experiences checklist, staff and residents had very different perceptions of the quality of life of the two groups, even on what appeared to be objective measures (Gentry, 1991). Residents were happy with their relationships, but not with opportunities, whereas staff felt that relationships were unsatisfactory in terms of ordinary life principles, but were devastated that their efforts in producing highly complex and individualised programmes were 'not appreciated'. It highlighted the importance of frequent examinations of interpretations of quality and the difficulty of setting standards. For example, what is to be said about a large number of choices residents can make when the only one they may wish to make is not available to them?

Recent developments in comprehensive quality assurance packages attempt to look at a range of views in relation to life in the home - Internal Quality Assurance. The Quartz system (1992) can also be a useful source of information to the inspector.

This system is a method of quality assurance which is designed for use by any mental health agency, using the experience and knowledge of staff and users. It was devised by a group of clinical psychologists within the Sainsbury Centre for Mental Health. *Inside Quality Assurance* (IQA) provides a means for residential homes to review and take stock of both what the home as a whole offers individuals and how it does this. It follows the recommendations of the Wagner group on choice and objectives. This review is carried out through a quality group consisting of representatives of residents, relatives, staff and of people from outside the home, one of whom will act a chairperson. The focus of the review is on the views of residents and there is a practical format, information and prompt cards to achieve this.

Residents' participation in committees and advisory panels

Residents' committees can be a source of gaining views but often owe more to the staff and manager's commitment than the residents themselves. There may be a genuine desire on the part of the manager to involve residents who 'have no interest' or the committee may simply be a flagship for viewing by the inspector. Any committee should represent the views of those to whom it is accountable, but conflicts arise in every field from cricket to toddler groups. There is the risk of substituting the committee view for the views of residents as individuals or collectively.

Residents should be well informed about the activities of advisory panels where they will not only be given the opportunity of expressing their views about the work of the inspection unit, but also about standards of care. Training may enable people to participate fully. As discussed in Chapter Eight the Department of Health's (1994b, 1994c) circular and Practice Guidance place increased emphasis on the participation of users and carers.

RESIDENTS AND LAY ASSESSORS

The introduction of lay assessors into the inspection process will offer the opportunity of a closer relationship between the resident and a 'non statutory' person. The reports of lay assessors, which should include the views of residents will help to improve knowledge of quality of life in the home. The purpose of lay assessment is to bring a non professional approach to the work of inspection, making 'a distinct contribution from the perspective of users, families and the wider community' (Department of Health, 1994b, para.11).

AIDS TO COMMUNICATION

Inspectors need to recognise the importance of equality of opportunity in obtaining the views of residents; they have a responsibility to seek to address communication difficulties by making use of a range of methods and ensuring that there are appropriate aids available: the use of interpreters for deaf people, communication through pictorial means, and various mechanical and technical aids. It is so easy to seek the views of the articulate resident while ignoring those who have communication difficulties.

For those in residential homes who have no obvious means of communication, in particular those with profound and multiple disabilities, attention will focus on indicators such as care plans to ensure that people are adhering to the principles of care. Experience shows that there are very few individuals who do not communicate; the difficulty is listening and comprehending. The inspector may need to communicate via the person who knows an individual best who may be a member of staff. This is a specific example of the fact that no information is ever free of context: people determine what they wish to say because of a number of factors. These include the items we have discussed such as feelings of vulnerability, concerns as to what they think others want them to say, anxiety about their dependence on people providing care or their own feelings on a particular occasion. In this example, the inspector will be aware of the fact that the person chosen by the resident (or been chosen for her/him) is a staff member.

PUTTING THE INFORMATION IN CONTEXT

Information from the resident must be viewed in the context of the ambience of the home and the quality of care provided. Indicators within the home of the relationship between users and staff may be displayed by indicators of power differentials

60

such as carrying the keys, or separate toilets for staff and residents. Alternatively, the indicators may be much more subtle, such as staff always responding to requests from residents that they will deal with them 'later' or 'in a few minutes'. Control time and you control life.

Staff are often unprepared to acknowledge that they are in a position of power and influence over residents. They may see themselves as caring friends and fail to recognise that the very closeness and gratitude of the resident for this relationship may be the most powerful tool in maintaining the status quo rather than enabling residents to express their wishes about the care they receive. The 'poor dear souls' or 'my residents' culture can be as restricting to freedom of expression as the openly authoritarian manager. The inspector will need to listen to what is not said by residents as well as what is said by staff.

There are arrangements in a home which develop so that a group of people can function together. Residents are perceptive of the unwritten rules of a home. These usually are indicative of the power of staff over day to day life in the home. Staff disapproval is an effective management technique. It is often these rules that residents feel least able to influence. Several examples of this style of influence are found in Clough's (1981) study of a home for older people, as when residents formally were told that they could call on the night staff at any time but informally, from the way staff talked about residents, picked up cues that night staff did not like to be bothered (p.161).

CONCLUSION

The destination of information given by residents should have been made clear to them and guidance given during the preparation period of the inspection as to the way the inspector will feedback relevant information to them, to the manager and to other staff. Written reports of the inspection should be available to all who can obtain access to them and of course can read and comprehend them.

Homes often are criticised for failing to produce an accessible complaints procedure but the task of feeding back information on the inspection visits is another that falls between the manager and inspector. It is amazing the small number of words of plain English into which a report can be condensed. As an announced annual inspection report is available for public consumption, there is no reason why a condensed report cannot be sent to all interested parties - residents, relatives, friends, advocates.

Most inspectorates recognise that it is important for the manager to be given time to reflect and feedback on the report. However, it is equally important that residents are visited to check that their views are adequately represented.

Inspecting residential care homes is a process of monitoring and evaluating and the views of users are crucial to both. External monitoring requires easy access to the inspector; internal monitoring may be carried out in a home which believes in internal quality measures. The emphasis in the inspection process on physical standards and compliance with legislation needs to be replaced by the more balanced approach which gives a greater say to the views of residents; in time, this will lead to improvements in care practice and influence quality of life in the home. There cannot be any substitute for residents' involvement in how the home is run. Evaluation of the home will reflect the inspection unit's interpretation of standards from legislation and its own practice guidance. It is essential that we listen also to the residents' views of what standards they want. Quality needs to be seen in relative as opposed to absolute terms.

A positive aspect of the inspection process is that it does often elucidate information of which staff and managers are genuinely unaware. The purpose of obtaining the views of residents is not only to address the power imbalance between service providers and receivers but also make maximum use of the information provided by residents to improve quality of life for all within the home.

Four

Learning from children and young people

Andrew Barbier with Roger Clough

INTRODUCTION

THIS CHAPTER follows the theme of the last insofar as it is an examination of users' views of services. However, the focus changes form that of finding out from users their views of the facility being inspected to assessing the user's views of the inspectorate. The material is drawn from a small scale research study conducted in Cumbria and concentrates on young people in boarding schools (Barbier, 1994).

The aim of the project was to answer the following question: 'What do young people living in boarding schools in Cumbria expect of Cumbria Social Services Inspectorate?' 'Young people' were taken to be anybody, male or female, under the age of eighteen (although some could be aged nineteen in their final year of the 6th form). 'Boarding schools' were defined as those schools where young people live and are educated away from their home base. The reason I undertook this research was to find out, in the section of the inspectorate in which I work, what the young people think of and expect from the inspectorate. One of the main problems that the project tried to address is that we do not know what young people think about inspection. For instance, 'Is our performance good enough? Are we effective? Do we improve the quality of life for young people?'

The background is important: the inspectorate is a relatively new organisation and has faced considerable change since its inception in 1990; substantial further changes had been proposed when this project was being undertaken such as introduction of lay assessors and the proposed reduction in frequency of inspections in large boarding schools.

Included in the Cumbria Social Services Inspectorate Business Plan for 1993-1994 (Cumbria County Council, 1993a) was the following statement: 'The public needs to be assured that the Inspectorate will deliver a high quality, consistent and reliable service'. The following year's plan, in a section on improvements to the service, notes that: 'methods of giving the views of users and carers about the role and practice of CSSI (Cumbria Social Services Inspectorate) will be developed, including 'enhancing' the role within Consultative Forums and Advisory Groups' (Cumbria County Council, 1994).

At interview when I joined the inspectorate in 1993, candidates were asked to give a presentation on the part the inspectorate might play in the empowerment of young people. That question stayed in my mind and was the main reason for doing this research. We may think that we empower young people, but is that the reality? Is there a gap between what inspectors and their managers consider is achieved and what young people actually know to happen? Do we communicate effectively with young people and hear their views, or do we just scratch the surface and deal with minor issues? Is the service we deliver of value for young people and worth all the time and expense?

At the time when the research was carried out, inspectors had completed the second round of inspections of every boarding and special school in Cumbria. It seemed an appropriate time to undertake some market research and find out if the work was proving effective: 'Were we achieving our aims and were there ways to improve our service?'

The study relied on qualitative information rather than quantitative: it examines people's perceptions by talking to them and analysing data rather than by asking them to tick or rate performance of inspectors and then quantifying the responses. Chisnall (1991) writes:

> Depth interviews are one of the principal methods of obtaining qualitative research, and are non-directive, informal interviews (more conservative in nature than traditional interviews) in which respondents are encouraged to talk about the subject rather than provide 'yes' or 'no' answers to specific questions (p.44).

The interviews were intended to be relaxed and thus enable sensitive, subjective topics to be discussed in ways which would explore people's attitudes. I wanted young people to have some opportunity to direct the meetings.

I decided to interview the young people in focus groups. A focus group is described as 'a derivation of group depth interviewing and has been used to explore user behaviour'. (Chisnall, 1991, p.44). In addition I interviewed four members of the inspectorate staff. A group of young people were interviewed in each of four schools, with another inspector present as observer. The four schools were all very different in character; the first was a mixed preparatory school for children up to 13 years; the second was a large boarding school for girls; the third was a large special school for boys with learning difficulties and the last was a small, special school for boys and girls, with behavioural and learning difficulties.

Obtaining permission to interview the young people was a sensitive matter as it had to be separated out from the job of inspecting the schools. I had to make it clear that I was wanting young people to talk about their opinions about the inspectorate and not about the schools. In one particular case I was asked to supply a copy of the taped interview to the school.

THE VIEWS OF YOUNG PEOPLE ABOUT RESIDENTIAL
LIFE AND INSPECTION

The background

There has been little, if any, work done on the views of service users about inspection. There is a significant amount of research into what users feel about their quality of life in the establishments they live in, in particular in residential homes for older people. The Department of Health's (1989) report *Homes are for Living In* presents material on the quality of life experienced in residential homes for older people.

A companion document has been produced entitled *School Life* which sets out young people's views on life in boarding schools and the implications for inspections. (Department of Health, 1993b) It does not however comment on the performance of inspectors. This is not surprising as boarding schools have only been inspected by social services departments in the last two years. In the preface to *School Life* Laming writes that 'a key principle of the Children Act is that the views of the children and young people should be actively sought and considered in matters affecting them'. In the overview to the research Morgan states 'the material in this book is offered on the basis that a primary source of information on which to base welfare standards for pupils in boarding schools should be the views and wishes of young people themselves'. *School Life* focused primarily on the standards young people would set for their own schools. It is interesting that the standards expected are similar to the six welfare issues in *Homes are for Living* in: privacy, dignity, independence, choice, rights and fulfilment. Where there were differences in the standards expected by pupils, these were accounted for more by the variations in what young people of different ages wanted than by differences between pupils from various schools.

At the end of *School Life* there is some discussion of what young people were expecting from the inspection process itself.

The 'best buy' Inspector is clearly someone who is trusted, visits unannounced, spends most of his or her time with pupils, who then forms his or her own independent opinion, respects confidences but can get things done if he or she decides anything needs changing.

The views on inspection of young people interviewed

The views of the young people have been summarised under a series of headings, each of which is examined in turn.

1. The reasons why the school is inspected

Most young people understood the reasons that their schools were inspected. They did not, as might be expected, have a detailed knowledge of the legislation that brought this into place, but in the answers given showed a remarkable insight into the process. There was only one young person that actually said he did not know why inspectors visited.

The following quotations are typical of the reasons young people gave for inspection:

> To find out how we get on.
>
> To see if we get on with each other and the staff.
>
> To iron out problems.
>
> To check we are being treated properly.
>
> To check we are fed properly and we are not starving.
>
> To try and make the place a better place to live in.
>
> To make sure we are not being beaten up.

2. Do young people feel able to talk to inspectors?

All young people spoken to within the focus groups said that they felt able to speak to inspectors. The question of what they felt able to talk about varied with the confidence of the young person, the skill of the inspectors at approaching young people, the frequency of meetings of inspectors and young people, and whether the young people interviewed had had a chance to speak to inspectors.

Particular comments were:

> I like the way the inspectors dress.
>
> We can speak to them because of their kindness.
>
> If you say things that are bad about the school they are not going to mention your name to the teachers.
>
> You could speak to them if you were upset.
>
> If we got to know the inspectors better we would be willing to talk.
>
> I wanted to speak to an inspector but didn't get the opportunity.
>
> Haven't really seen any inspectors.
>
> They were friendlier on this last inspection.

Young people felt they could approach inspectors, but pointed out that they wanted to get to know them better. Some preferred to be on their own when they spoke to inspectors, whereas others wanted their friends present. Most remembered the individual inspectors even after two years, some by looks, some by name.

3. What is the best way for young people to give their opinions to inspectors?

It is important to note that in the four schools pupils had experienced different ways of being asked their opinions. All had completed a standard questionnaire in the first round of inspections. In the second year new methods were added: some were given the opportunity to write letters rather than complete questionnaires and inspectors met with certain young people in small groups. Informal contact had taken place at all schools with some children, for example at meals and other social occasions.

Most of the young people wanted to have a variety of ways

to communicate with the inspectors. There were those who preferred to fill in questionnaires as these were anonymous, whereas one boy said he would rather talk to inspectors in a small group as he found it difficult to write. Many asked to be seen in groups after school time. One person said she had spoken to an inspector on a one to one basis and it had really helped her. The young people were pleased that they could telephone inspectors if they wanted to but many felt serious problems were usually dealt with by their school in the first instance. The letters, used by inspectors on the second round of inspections, do not appear to have gone down very well. As one person said, 'You automatically think of bad points, in the letter, as it depends on what is going on in the school at the time'.

4. Do young people think it is worth speaking to inspectors?

The majority of young people said it was worth speaking to inspectors but that it depended on the nature of the matter raised whether anything got done. Certainly some of the young people appeared to expect inspection to lead to change:

> I don't think anything has been done about what you said.

> A lot was done about the school before you got here.

> If it was major it would be sorted out in school.

The other striking aspect of the responses is the importance of inspectors as confidantes:

> At the time it feels better to speak, it gets the aggro out.

> Nice to talk to someone out of school about problems – and to someone who actually listens.

> Inspectors give sensible advice.

> We can talk to you lot 'cos you just come and go.

> You understand us sometimes.

Whether or not this function will decrease in significance as other channels are opened, for example with independent visitors, remains to be seen.

5. Do young people see a copy of the inspectorate report?

Without exception, all the young people spoken to said 'No!'. The more able pupils very quickly connected this to answers to other questions and said, 'We do not know whether anything is done as a result of your visit as we don't know what the report says'. There is an element of frustration here for the young people who have participated in the inspection (or at least seen it happen around them) and then do not know the results:

> It would be nice to find out what you have said and what you thought about the school.

> Everybody just presumes you thought it was all right and that was it.

> It is not discussed with us afterwards.

6. The times and frequency of inspectors' visits to schools

All the young people who participated in this project wanted inspectors to visit their schools more often. There were lots of suggestions as to the time of year that would be most suitable and whether inspectors should visit the schools without warning:

> ...visit at night time; come twice per year; come in the summer and see more fun and games; once per term; easier to talk to us if you come more often; doesn't matter doesn't make any difference; one planned, one surprise; the more times inspectors visit, the more open and confident people would be speaking to them.

The majority of young people wanted inspectors to visit at different times of the year and to visit the school without warning.

7. Have young people seen any changes to the fabric of their school as a result of inspections?

As four very different schools were visited a variety of points were mentioned. Most of the children said that substantial changes had taken place:

One house has closed.

Every time you come something gets better.

A telephone box has been put in.

We wouldn't know, if we didn't know what was wrong.

Dormitories are less crowded.

There are new chairs and tables.

There are new beds, the dorms have been decorated.

8. Have young people seen a change in their quality of life as a result of inspections?

As with the previous topic, the responses varied depending on the school and the perceptions of each individual. In the main, young people thought that their 'quality of life' had improved and none thought it had got worse:

People do listen.

The atmosphere has been nicer.

Some staff have left.

Not as much aggro.

Feel we get noticed now when we do good and not just when we do wrong.

The School Council has been formed.

The school notices our problems quicker.

More done about it now if we complain.

There is a complaints book now.

More games time.

The increase in time for games was seen as positive, though presumably for others it might not have been so! However, there were some comments on increased safety measures: they wanted to know what and where they were, and did not want to feel either trapped or that they were 'wrapped in cotton wool'.

9. Suggestions for the improvement of inspections

As might be expected there were many suggestions,

especially as this was the last question and the young people by this time were more relaxed and forthcoming. Some proposals for improvements had been mentioned in earlier questions. There were many points made about the frequency and duration of visits, relating to opportunities to communicate more readily with inspectors. The range of views is highlighted below:

> Keep on going the way you are.
>
> Slacken-up. (This was a reference to dressing more casually).
>
> Thanks for keeping on coming.
>
> Talk in small groups, like this to us, as it is not good enough to just catch us at mealtimes.
>
> Spend more time speaking to us – like you are doing now.
>
> Stay for a longer time.
>
> Come more often.
>
> Come back to talk to us about the report.
>
> Join us in activities and we can talk to you more.
>
> Put in a good word for us.
>
> Not enough time spent with us this year.
>
> Don't just come in class forms, see us in activity times.
>
> If you say something has to be done, keep on coming and checking it has been done.

The views of inspectors

The perceptions of inspectors, in the main, were similar to those of the young people, a significant finding in itself. Rather than cover the ground again question by question I have selected topics. Again, in large measure the comments of inspectorate staff are allowed to stand on their own.

1. On the ease with which young people talk to inspectors

> It depends on how inspectors present themselves; it depends how the school presents the inspectors; it

depends on what opportunities are available to meet with inspectors; and it depends on the disposition of each individual.

2. Methods of communicating with young people

The questionnaire is the best way to get a wide span of opinion; it prompts children to talk.

Another inspector thought that the questionnaire can limit what young people want to say and the letter allowed for freer narrative. It was also pointed out that a questionnaire was not easy to complete for children with learning difficulties:

'Seeing young people out of the school setting, when socialising with each other and joining in with them in a relaxed setting, rather than a formal level.

We have not got it right yet; maybe we need a combination of all sorts of things.

3. On whether it is worth young people's time to talk to inspectors

A balance is important, we need to be seen as effective but not just people who get the goodies.

Inspectors did not want to be seen as magicians:

Care needs to be taken not to raise unrealistic expectations.

The ideal is that young people should feel able to talk to their staff group about things they want changing.

Not worried about children understanding who was responsible for change, the fact that change happens is enough.

4. Re young people's access to reports

We are often misquoted.

I would like to think it is available, at the moment they are not even advised of the main contents.

It was pointed out that the Inspectorate Advisory Panel was to consider how the reports could be made more widely available to both staff and pupils.

5. Frequency of inspectorate visits

If we went more frequently young people would be more confident in who we were and what we were about; however if we went too often it would break down our objectivity and would be intrusive.

The devilment in them would like us to go unannounced and catch the school out; this is a fantasy that some young people have.

6. On changes to buildings or life-style

All the inspectors said that young people would see changes to the fabric of the building as a result of inspections. They all had evidence of this based on what pupils had told them during inspections or what they had heard reported:

Some of the changes we might have influenced may not be obvious to the young people, particularly if they don't see our reports.

A number of schools have made significant changes either directly as a result of us or coincidentally as they were going to make the changes anyway.

We have all felt that the actual level of response to our recommendations has actually been high.

There are changes and they are as much to do with the fact we are around as to what we have actually said; the fact we are going along is a catalyst.

Not sure the children attribute change to us, and not fussed either way; the fact is the schools have actually taken things on board and are doing something about it. I am not in the business of scoring points.

Hopefully a lot of schools were running well in the first place.

It would be preferable that the young people thought

the changes came about because the school management were receptive to them, rather than the inspectors had had to come and change it.

I am not aware of hard evidence that young people see an improvement.

Nevertheless in the view of most of the Inspectors the 'quality of life' has altered significantly:

A complaints procedure exists where it didn't before is progress in itself.

We have to remember that we are still in the early stages of the inspectorate as a body and, in the main, we are not going to bring about change overnight. The fact we have developed positive relationships leaves the door open for further changes being made and youngsters will benefit greatly, but it will take time.

7. On future developments for the inspectorate

We need to make ourselves more available to young people, for them to get used to us, and to get more of their views, not only the complaints but the good things.

Hit on a more open style of working with children e.g. a surgery at school, especially a big school, a bit like a live 'suggestion box'.

Time scale is an issue for us as it comes down to resourcing.

Feedback to the young people and staff at the end of inspections, not just the head teachers.

We need to review our standards in the light of our experience of inspections, and the way we approach the job in the light of feedback from young people, the schools and the experience of the Inspectors.

We need another dialogue with the schools, (not just the Advisory Panel) about practice two years on and an occasional forum with staff and pupils to ask them what we should do differently.

6. The proposals to reduce the frequency of inspections

I'm concerned about reducing the level of inspections because we are not able to spend sufficient time in the schools at the moment.

To get under the skin of an institution is quite difficult and takes time.

The trust we have built up with schools and young people will be affected by reducing the number and quality of inspections (as proposed). Both are under threat, the former by changes in the guidance and the latter by the possible reduction in resources to the inspectorate.

Personally I am very disappointed at the prospect of moving to one inspection every four years; it is a travesty, having spent all of this time and energy setting it all up to find ourselves in a very short space of time contradicting it all.

In Cumbria we may not have got it all right but we have built up a good relationship with schools; we have not had the confrontations that have brought about this circular; it is very sad, and very much a backward step.

CONCLUSIONS

One particular aspect of the stress placed in this chapter on communication is worth highlighting because it is discussed little elsewhere: what are the ways by which inspectorates may communicate directly with their 'customers', rather than have their message filtered through another body. Typically, users get their perception of the function of inspection and indeed its usefulness from staff providing the service. This may have a significant effect on the interaction with inspectors when they arrive. At times users may want to be loyal to help staff whom they like; at others they may be uneasy as to the consequences of talking to inspectors. Inspectorates adopt various strategies: meeting with users before the start of an inspection; contact with users through advisory panels; sending letters or brochures direct to interested parties. Of course it must not be presumed that users want to spend time talking to inspectors.

In the larger schools, the young people were not sure how enough of them could get access to inspectors. The suggestion from inspectors of times of the day when they have an open door to anyone who wants to visit may be useful. There is also reference to the familiarity of inspectors: how far is it possible to provide continuity of personnel? Indeed, is continuity at times in conflict with the need to ensure that individual inspectors do not build up both close relationships and set views so that they find it hard to take in new information?

Another aspect of inspections is the mass of information which is produced: is it useful? is it the most important information? is there time to analyse it and to draw on it when assessing the quality of provision? For example, inspectorate staff found it difficult to process the interesting information that was produced in the questionnaires. In Cumbria the questionnaire is to be redesigned, probably being made shorter; easier to analyse and more relevant to all abilities. In addition there is to be a section to allow young people chance to comment on their views of the inspection process itself.

There is another issue here which needs clarifying between inspectorate staff, young people and the staff of the schools: to what extent is there an expectation that the consequence of raising a matter at an inspection will be that changes will follow? This is an important topic because there is potential for young people to bypass their usual methods of raising items and to use inspectors as vehicles for change. Of course, they may refer items to inspectors just because they have tried other means and had no success. The issue is whether a matter that is raised with inspectors does or should take precedence over other items.

An interesting theme to emerge was the value some young people found in being able to talk to outsiders. We do not have the information on the amount of contact that young people had with people from outside the school but it is apparent that for some the visits from the inspectors provided a valuable opportunity to talk.

The whole of this chapter needs to be seen in the context of a very early stage in the life of the inspectorate. Inspectors were aware that they were more relaxed on second visits because the different groups of young people, managers, staff and inspectors had met and seen the way in which inspections were carried out: some fantasies and fears had been dispelled. The concluding comment must be the overwhelming enthusiasm of the young people for contact with inspectors. The Government is caught between two interest groups and competing principles: heads of schools arguing for reduced frequency of inspection, reinforcing the move for reduction in regulation and bureaucracy; on the other hand, there is the principle of listening to service users who, in this small study, overwhelmingly endorsed increased inspection.

Five

Being an inspector

Roger Clough

INTRODUCTION

THE DEPARTMENT of Health (1994b) on the day that I am starting to write this chapter has issued its latest policy statement on 'Opening up inspections'. In brief, the requirement is that the work of the inspector will be opened up to scrutiny from lay people. This is an important issue which is touched on in different parts of this book. But it raises neatly the question of what is characteristic to the task and function of the inspector: how far has the inspector distinctive roles and responsibilities? how far is the inspector simply paid to carry out full time a task that others can do without training, and perhaps without recompense? are there skills that are special to inspection?

AMBIVALENCE TO REGULATION

Questions such as these could be multiplied. I want to start by acknowledging the ambivalence that exists towards regulation. However much the philosophy is preached of a free market which should regulate itself, a market in which poor providers go out of business because nobody wants to buy their goods, the reality is that there are circumstances in which successive governments have determined that costs should not fall where they lie. In other words there are circumstances where the buyer or the user is to be protected.

Thus, users of social care services are to be protected by regulation. It follows that users and their carers have expectations of inspectors. Imagine that you or someone you care about is considering a move into a residential home or is about to choose a day nursery or childminder. How do you know whether the place and the staff will be good? How can you assess what the quality of the provision will be and indeed try to work out whether you or your loved one will find the place satisfactory? Getting the appropriate information to make a choice is difficult enough for a very small event in our lives such as a holiday: you want to know about concrete factors such as the basic cost, the facilities and the extras but you also want to know about less tangible matters, perhaps the ambience, or the balance of quietness and activity. Faced with the difficulty, we may look helplessly at the assistant in the travel agent and ask for an opinion on the place, even though we know that this is of little help.

The problems of selection are hugely magnified for the person choosing social care services. The 'consumer' is likely to be making decisions at a time of distress or vulnerability, is more dependent on others for services, is less likely to be assertive and may have less energy to check out the quality of provision. However, the overriding differentiating factor is that the decision matters more because it is concerned with the fundamentals of our daily lives: for a residential home, the choice is about a combination of the place where you are to live, the people with whom you will live and the services you will get.

The minimum of what anybody will expect is that users of facilities will be safe from abuse. Sadly, in some places the provision is inadequate or even abusive. For reasons which are not the subject of this book, the very provision of services for vulnerable, troubled and perhaps troublesome people appears to result in some staff taking advantage of highly dependent and vulnerable users. Thus there is a proper expectation that regulation will prevent abuse.

To many, the notion of regulation in abstract seemed a good idea; indeed regulation was the justification for the encouragement of the expansion of independent sector residential homes. Yet the same government which created new powers and responsibilities for inspection units to tackle such issues also preaches deregulation. Business, we are told, is to be freed from the red tape and bureaucracy of inspection as much else.

Once again, the ambivalence is apparent. Regulation to protect vulnerable people appears an obvious good. However, the very act of protection involves specification. The specification will arouse concerns about the appropriateness of the detail. This is as true of inspection standards as it is of the national curriculum. As regulation is put into effect, standards are produced which specify criteria for registration and inspection. This specification of criteria results in an immediate dilemma since people will differ as to what should be included, be it the size of rooms or a ban on smoking by adults providing day care for children. The problem is solved neither by leaving matters to the discretion of the inspector with a phrase such as 'rooms of a reasonable size for their purpose' nor by specifying fine detail, for example defining the exact area of space for a resident's room or a bathroom. Regulation involves determining, by whatever process, that one facility meets requirements and another does not.

The Department of Health's (1994b, para.11) circular states that: 'lay assessors will complement the work done by professional inspectors. They can reinforce the importance of common sense observation...'. This reinforces the fallacy that there is a 'sensible' view if only inspectors would adopt it. Nearly always 'common sense' is used in this type of statement to mean the unspecified view of the writer which he/she wants to presume is shared by the majority of right thinking people. Regulation is very often good in abstract, good for another service or in another home or on another day. Ambivalence of all parties lies at the heart of inspection.

Imagine that you are about to arrive at a residential home or school, or at a day care facility for children under eight. You are going to undertake an inspection (whether as lay assessor or salaried inspector). Some of the issues which are going through your mind are parochial ('Have I got the right time and day?') while others are about your competence, authority or credibility. The owner or manager is likely to be ambivalent. Rationally most people will say that they do not mind anyone inspecting their work and indeed may say, and mean, 'Drop in any time'. But what we want from the inspection is a recognition of the high quality of our work. Howard Jacobson (1994) talking about reviews of his writing, has said that what he, as all writers, really wants is a review without limitations. A review which states that the book is very good, and is indeed the best book of its type to be published in England this year is not sufficient because of the limitation. Secretly he wants the review which recognises that he has written the best book of any type, in any age, in any language! Inspectors have to relate to the rational and the unconscious of the provider.

CHARACTERISTICS OF INSPECTION

Making assessments and judgements

A core characteristic of inspection is the judging of the work of others. The central task involves assessing the quality of activity. It may seem to others that the task is to try to catch people out, a function akin to that of the inspector on the London Underground who, according to a recent poster, will want to see either a ticket or the money for a fine. The social services inspector differs not only from that type of inspection, but also from the police and from child or adult protection staff. The comparisons are helpful to tease out the nature of social services inspection. The police aim both to prevent crime and to investigate whether a crime has been committed. The child or adult protection worker, similar in part to the function of the police, starts from suggestions of abuse, and has to examine whether these are demonstrated. If there are concerns, the worker has to consider what action should be taken. The tasks of inspectorates in social services have similarities to the work of the trading standards officers who may either carry out routine tests to determine whether specified standards and claims are being met or may examine complaints.

There are parallels also with all of these jobs concerning the characteristics of the work: is the skill a technical one reliant on massing and then sorting evidence? (There will be skills in determining what evidence to collect, where to look for it and what is the significance of what is found.) Or is the skill to be seen as an art, requiring imagination to understand and to question what appears on the surface? Developing from this are issues as to the nature of the expertise of the inspector. Is there a coherent knowledge base related to the task of inspection? In addition, there is a question as to the extent of knowledge needed by the inspector of the tasks being carried out at any facility subject to inspection. To be competent to inspect (and/or to be recognised to be competent) does the inspector have to be an expert cook, architect, builder, nurse, doctor, psychologist, manager and care worker?

The social services inspector has both to register and inspect. In the first function the task is to assess whether or not a facility meets set requirements In the second, as a routine task, the inspector has to assess the quality of provision. Most explicit statements would expect inspectorate staff 'to report on what is good as well as what is not so good', as did Cumbria Social Services Inspectorate (CSSI). In this respect the social services inspector has a function like that of the hotel assessor to report on the quality of the provision, not simply on whether it falls below minimum standards. Gibbs and Sinclair's study (1992a) raises questions as to the validity of inspectors' assessments of quality, as has been referred to in Chapter One. The issue is examined further in Chapters Six and Seven. For the time being there are two factors to be borne in mind; first, that providers are very dissatisfied with reports which state what is wrong without highlighting good aspects; secondly they dislike the best that can be achieved in the report as being 'satisfactory' or that 'minimum levels have been reached'. Standard advice on giving feedback specifies the importance of recognising what has been done well. It would seem that this should be the least of what an inspection report should be doing. Further, since reports are likely to be used increasingly by prospective purchasers, reports should aim to show the differences between facilities.

Because of the risks attached to getting judgements wrong, especially that of judging a place to be satisfactory when it later turns out to be appalling, there is a temptation for inspectors to avoid saying good things about a place. It seems a worse failing to have judged somewhere to be good and then to find out how bad it was than to have merely stated that it was 'satisfactory'. Acknowledging high performance is risky, but essential.

Many social services inspectors will describe the tension between a) wanting to support staff in facilities, b) making judgements about performance and c) taking action when performance is unsatisfactory. In this there are parallels with the child protection worker (and to a much lesser extent the police) who want to help families stay together, to support parents through times of stress and to safeguard the welfare of young people.

Uneasiness with 'inspection'

Several inspectors have said to me that they have been worried that an emphasis on inspection may destroy their relationships with the staff of the facility. Some describe their 'real work' or the work to which they attach most value as that of development. I think that this view is mistaken. For whatever reason, inspectorate staff may be unwilling to recognise what lies at the heart of their work. Perhaps it is hard to acknowledge that the bottom line of one's work is regulation: 'development' or 'support' may seem more acceptable as central activities to people who may have come into social service activity with the intention of 'helping others'. Similarly Wing (1992, p.77) writes that: 'Until recently the word inspection has been considered taboo within the personal social services. Instead of "inspection" several other words have been used, for example monitoring, evaluation, review, quality control, audit, appraisal'.

Of course no activity exists without a context. The act of meeting the people who are providing the facility which is to be inspected inevitably results in some type of relationship between inspector and inspected. The nature of that relationship is important yet is hard to specify. What degree of friendliness or familiarity is appropriate to the task of inspection? When is the inspector, treated as a guest, honoured visitor or friend, led (or seduced) into a position from which it is harder to be disciplined about a judgement or to determine what action to be taken? Alternatively, is the 'friendly' inspector consciously or unconsciously trying to lull staff into a position of a false security only to use the information gained in ways which staff had not expected. I remember as a researcher as I thought making an explicit statement at the beginning of a study that my task was to understand what it was like to live and work in a residential home. Yet later, some staff were hurt when I reported my conclusions gleaned in part from sitting around and observing while being unobtrusive and pleasant. I think that I was seen as a snake in the grass.

The purpose of the inspector's visit is that of checking. It is no good trying to disguise that and indeed it is essential that the 'checking' aspect of the task is explicit. It is not just the person being inspected who may wish to fudge the task. The inspector may wish to present an image to the world to soften the 'inspecting' or 'checking' function. Indeed, it may be that the inspector wants to see her or himself as more nurturing than inspecting allows.

Not taking what is said or seen at face value

There is another fundamental aspect of the task, inherent in the word 'checking' that raises questions about central values. The inspector is not to take at face value what is said.

Instead, for example when a manager says that particular sorts of action are taken when a complaint is received, the task is to acknowledge the statement but to explain that the evidence for it has to be seen by the inspector. This has immense significance for the nature of the relationships with those being inspected and for the inspector's own perception of her/his work. A trust has to be established between different parties that the task of inspection will be carried out with integrity but the trust is not that of accepting what is said until there is information to the contrary, which as individuals is what we are encouraged to do in so much of our lives. By contrast, the inspector must keep critical faculties to the fore rather than have them lurking beneath the surface so that she/he is alert to the clues which exist. I am not sure that the phrase 'being suspicious' quite captures the approach I am trying to describe. It is not as simple as doubting what is said or written: it is a combination of wanting to see evidence and being willing to doubt. Indeed, once there is a suspicion or doubt there is a necessity to search for information to support or question the doubt.

I remember at an inspection by Home Office inspectors of an approved school where I worked a special event being put on one evening. 'How often do you have activities like this?', the inspector asked one of the boys. 'The first one since I have been here' was the inevitable reply. That is an obvious, and comparatively insignificant, example of what I mean. The inspector had to get a picture of life in the school; presumably he knew that he would see a snapshot – specific events at particular moments. So he has to know how typical the event is of life in the establishment if the report is to be of any value. How is the inspector to get beneath the surface and to discover whether the glossy brochure or the surface picture is accurate?

It is equally important that worrying events are seen in context. Is the staff member shouting at a resident indicative of a pervasive culture in which that particular worker (or all workers) treat residents with minimal respect? Or is it that this person provides good and sensitive care for residents but at this time is over tired or angry at a particular incident?

Nevertheless, this characteristic, perhaps best seen as both 'the suspension of a willingness to trust the accuracy of what is stated' and 'the conscious enhancement of critical faculties' has consequences for the inspector. The day to day work of the inspector is to suspend belief and to search for evidence. The strangeness of that needs to be remembered, and has implications for support and training. Inspectors may not be conscious of this and, of course, may avoid it. But this characteristic, when carried out properly, has implications for both work life and for personal life. The work demands a style of checking that is not easily left behind as the front door is closed on the facility being inspected.

Repetitive tasks: Becoming stale or staying fresh

Often inspection in social services is repetitive. This is more so in inspection of childminders than any other groups where the sheer volume of the task means that the activity may be repeated daily or more frequently. However, inspectors of residential care will carry out large numbers of inspections in a year, the numbers dropping only where there may be comparatively few facilities (as is the case with community homes for children and young people) or when the size of the task makes the inspection longer and shared with a team, as with a large independent sector residential school. As with any other repetitive job, there is an issue as to how to ensure that inspectors stay alert. A further hazard is that of boredom, with its related danger that inspectors may approach the job in a certain way to generate excitement to relieve monotony.

There is a further consequence to going back to the same place that has been inspected on other occasions. The inspector starts the later inspection with knowledge of the findings and the judgements from previous inspections. Thus there will be a framework for the current inspection. There is a history or 'career' to the inspection of each place. It will be known, for example, that at the last inspection or, indeed, inspections the overall assessment of the facility was that this was a good place with some factors recommended for improvement or that there were major anxieties about certain practices, even though there had been some good aspects. The danger for the inspector is that the previous knowledge may blunt the perception to current evidence.

However sound the previous assessment of the inspector, the current picture may be very different. The quality of care in residential homes and day care facilities may change markedly in a short space of time and, in particular, it may deteriorate rapidly. One of the reasons for this is the significant effect on the quality of provision of the manager or owner of the facility; major events in the life of the leader may influence his/her capacity to oversee the arrangements of the establishment. Once the leader's interest diminishes, other staff may become less concerned about the minutiae of practice. Provision of care for others, more than most jobs, is dependent on one's own emotional state. At times when one feels vulnerable and perhaps in need of care for oneself, it may be immensely difficult to acknowledge the needs of others and to provide for the meeting of those needs. These problems may be nearer to the surface and have a significant effect on the whole life of the place if there are profound tensions between co-owners or managers who have also been partners in the sense of being married or living together.

For all these reasons inspectors have to find ways continually to stay fresh and be alert: the questioning and searching from the last visit will influence but must not determine the approach of the inspector on the current visit. However, the need for a fresh approach on each occasion does not result in its happening. And the likelihood is that the place which was satisfactory last time will be good enough on this occasion. This probability makes it even harder to stay alert. What I am trying to describe is a type of extension of the attitude described earlier of not taking statements or events at face value: the inspector has to develop a working relationship with the owners or managers of the facility; in effect (s)he has to say, 'Not only will I want to see the evidence for myself on the first inspection, but I shall want to repeat the process on successive inspections.' It is a continuing, and permanent, attitude of not taking information on trust.

Getting to know a place and the people who work there is likely to lead to an increasingly full picture. Certainly, whether justified or not, longer acquaintance will make the inspector think that he/she has greater knowledge, though the reality may be that all that is happening is a reinforcement of that first view. The task is to build up an increasingly reliable picture based on additional evidence and to find a way to suspend reliance on that perspective so that there is a continuing awareness of the importance of being alive to contra-indications. Going back to an establishment for successive inspections has the potential both for getting better information and for being sucked into a view of the place that is hard to shift. There is a value in involving other people in inspections whether through joint inspections with colleagues or through lay assessors.

Emotional forces: delivering 'truth', telling people off and having authority

There are powerful emotional forces at work in inspections. The first arises from the expectation that inspection should be an absolute, setting out what a facility is really like. The phrase 'setting out what a facility is like' suggests that there is truth and that the issue is whether the inspector is able to reveal that truth. There are immense pressures on inspectorates to presume to themselves and others that they are competent to describe the place as it really is and to imagine that they alone are in a position to define 'the real thing'. Users, relatives, staff, managers and 'the public' all realise that it is difficult to know what goes on when they are not at the home or day care facility; what they want from the inspectorate is a picture which may be relied upon. It is reasonable to expect the inspectorate to be reliable but not to presume that it will provide complete truth or objectivity.

It may be possible, given enough supporting evidence, for inspectors to come to a firm conclusion about the quality of care or about a particular incident, for example stating that relationships between staff and residents are caring and friendly or, that in the view of the inspectorate, a resident has been hit by a staff member. Indeed, from the evidence the inspectorate may conclude that the hitting of residents is pervasive in the culture of a particular place and that, in its judgement, the establishment should be closed down. But firm conclusions differ from the absolute expected from 'truth' or even 'objectivity'; perhaps what is required is what Beedell (1983) has referred to as 'disciplined subjectivity', a phrase used in relation to assessment to describe the requirement that staff should be rigorous in their work but could not (and should not) be expected to be objective, with the suggestion of being outside the event.

Inspectors have to avoid the expectation that they will be able to deliver truth. In fact they provide a perspective. Hopefully, that perspective will be valuable and reliable for a number of reasons: they have no direct interests in the business or management of the organisation; from a variety of sources (including present and former training) they have skills in observation and assessment; they have knowledge of the required standards and of their statutory responsibility; perhaps most importantly they have an understanding of the nature of day and residential provision, with an understanding of the characteristics of what leads to good care and what results in poor care.

The second strong emotional force arises from the nature of examining the work of others. At the heart of inspection is the act of checking for conformity with what people claim and with specified standards. The task is not to catch people out, though it may feel like that to those being inspected and some inspectors may act as if that is the case. But the core expectation on the inspector to check on the work of others leads to deep seated recollections of occasions when someone in authority has judged one's performance to be poor. The most obvious example of this is the child with its parents, with its strong desire to please and be thought well of. The child is anxious that it may fail to please either because it knows it has not done what was expected or because it did not know what was expected. We would all recognise feelings of apprehension associated with a teacher approaching us as pupils (or for some as parents at Parents' evenings at school!), a police officer flagging us down even though we were not aware of breaking any law or perhaps a line manager asking to have a word with us in the office. Inspection by its very nature, and however well managed by inspector and inspected, arouses trace memories of such events. Inevitably those being inspected will resent such reminders.

In addition, consciously or unconsciously the inspector/ staff relationship may reflect the staff/user relationship in which the staff member is providing services for someone who is able to manage few daily care tasks and therefore is dependent on the staff member.

Inspectors have vested in them considerable authority. One of the keys to successful inspection is to acknowledge and to be at ease with the existence of authority and to be aware of its significance. Once again powerful forces come into play not only for those being inspected but also for inspectors: there are the memories of occasions when you wanted to get your own back on those in authority, together with the fantasies of how you would do it; there are the doubts of your own ability to exercise authority. The job requires something of a terrier like checking of doubts. I think that it also produces an excitement which has its parallels in aspects of child protection work, particularly on occasions when a serious matter is being investigated. The inspector is at the centre of events with information, responsibility and power. It seems incongruous or insensitive for inspectors to have a buzz of excitement at times when the task is to examine whether residents have been abused and when the outcome of the investigation may have immense consequences for numerous people. Yet I think that the excitement is a part of the reason why people are attracted to the work and should be recognised so that the inspector is not carried away by titillation.

Anxieties and risks in making judgements

There are anxieties for inspectorate staff that follow from the responsibilities of the tasks. Inspectors too fear getting things wrong, in their case through missing vital clues, being hoodwinked or drawing the wrong conclusions. When malpractice is revealed to have taken place, consequent reports from an investigating team may reveal that an inspectorate had visited and had not recorded any concerns. Indeed, there is a strong expectation, if not a requirement, that inspectorates will make their reports publicly available. This is already current practice in many authorities. The consequence is that the work of inspectors is widely available for scrutiny by the general public and those with a direct interest: managers, owners, users, relatives, councillors. *Inspecting Social Services* contains specific references to open reporting.

The earlier policy guidance included a requirement to make inspection reports publicly available subject to legal advice. That requirement is now re-emphasised. Authorities should take steps to make sure as far as possible that those most directly affected by and interested in reports know of their existence and how they can obtain copies. Copies should also normally be supplied in response to any request from a member of the public (Department of Health, 1994b, para.28).

Not only will comparisons be made on the seeming equity of reports on different establishments but the judgements will be scrutinised as well. I have noted already the potential for people to want to rely on the judgements of the inspectorate, and thus to hold inspectorates to account if those judgements turn out to be mistaken. The other side of the coin is that many people think that there are no real skills in inspection. Frequently when talking about inspection to people who are not inspectors I have been told, 'I know as soon as I go through the front door whether or not a place is all right'. To that extent everyone is an inspector, second guessing the conclusions of the inspector.

Collecting the evidence: not relying on intuition, not rushing to conclusions, developing hypotheses

Inspectors collect information. They have to put aside the instinct or intuition that others may claim gives them an insight into the quality of life. They do this not so much because they mistrust such attributes but because they have to have evidence for their conclusions. Their task is to search for the factors on which the intuition is built up, to find the tangible which underlies what is presumed to be intangible. It is almost as if the inspector tries to stand outside of him or herself and use her or himself as an instrument for examining what is happening in the place. A singer has to learn to view the voice as an instrument on which tunes are to be played as if she/he is external to the voice. As with any other instrument the task is to get the instrument to play in the way you want. It is in this sense that the inspector has to try to be external to his or her experiences. The mind is using everything that happens to compile a picture: 'I am beginning to think about this place that... ; from what am I getting that impression? how do I examine further or check my ideas or feelings?' The inspector has to be aware of his or her impressions but to remain agnostic to them, perhaps to treat them as if they were someone else's views which are to be considered but not automatically adopted.

One of the essentials for the inspector is not to rush to an early conclusion. For as long as is reasonable the inspector is to collect information, of which her/his own impressions are a part. The timing of this stage must vary with the type of inspection and the sorts of impressions that are emerging. There are of course occasions when it is essential to formulate a view promptly so that urgent action may be taken. Thus various stages of inspection may be identified though they are bound to overlap: collecting information; forming a hypothesis; finding ways to search for supportive and contrary evidence; reaching a judgement about the quality of the provision; determining what action is to be taken; reporting back to the manager. What I have tried to suggest is that the inspector should use his or her own feelings and impressions as part of the collecting information stage, artificially trying to see the first hints of the hypotheses also as part of that stage.

A second essential is to ensure that a hypothesis is developed. Inspection, as any task which requires someone to come to a conclusion about the quality of provision, exposes the inspector to risks, for the judgement will be made public and may prove to be faulty. So there is a temptation to put off that judgement. Indeed, there may be a perverse hope that the judgement will not have to be made on the grounds that massing together enough information will lead to the conclusion emerging as a self evident statement. It is like hoping that an essay (or book!) will write itself if only I read enough books and have enough notes. Whatever quantity of information is obtained, a judgement still has to be made by the inspector. Check lists, however sophisticated, do not provide an escape for the inspector, in part because judgement is often required to answer the question on the checklist about the adequacy of specific facilities, but mainly because the inspector's task is to put the information collected into an overview, and it is that overview that requires the exercise of judgement.

Telling stories

This judgement of the inspector is the kernel of the task. The inspector must manage doubts and certainties. This involves checking by searching for further evidence. But the doubts and certainties have to be put into perspective. This aspect of the judgement of the inspector perhaps is best understood by considering the way in which the inspector will tell the story of the inspection. I do not intend to trivialise the work by referring to the telling of stories. But that is what the process comprises. As with the telling of all stories the inspector has to determine: from whose perspective is the story to be told? is the conclusion to come at the beginning with the rest of the narrative giving a perspective (the evidence)? what information is the reader to be given? how much detail is to be included? and so on. However, the most significant aspect of this analogy is the recognition that the story teller is not neutral, however much there is the pretence of being an impartial observer. The story teller's framework plays a major part in the reader's view of events. The way the story is told is likely to influence whether the characters are seen as good (with flaws) or bad (perhaps with some redeeming features).

The same two aspects apply to the inspector. First, the evidence has to be put into the context of an overall assessment of the place: 'good' or 'good enough' with some faults or 'unsatisfactory' with some good points. And, secondly, the inspector must ensure that the overall assessment is taking account of the totality of the information and does not derive from a pre-judgement.

CONCLUSION

Inspection in social care carries some of the same tensions and requires some of the same skills as inspection in any other field. All inspection has elements that are technical (knowing the standards and nature of the inspector's authority, being aware of tests cases, collecting information) and elements that require judgement (does this particular example match the specification?). Social care inspection has specific elements:

- the inspection assessment or judgement relates to the quality of life provided for users of services, a concept which is difficult to define and runs the risk of being subjective;
- the users of services are likely to be vulnerable before using the service and dependent on providers for significant aspects of their daily care;
- some people will hide their sadness, despair or anger at the way in which they are treated;
- the feelings encountered in inspection touch deep, central feelings about self: our worth as individuals; the ways in

which care demonstrates the feelings of others towards us; our own futures; our relationships with others.

Inspection in social care needs the skills of the scientist and of the artist, for people must be meticulous and test evidence thoroughly on the one hand and yet, on the other, make creative leaps about what it would be like to live in that place and use imagination in searching for clues. In addition it is vital that inspectors recognise the significance of feelings: the feelings aroused by intimate, physical care for users and providers of services; the strong and deep feelings about oneself and one's worth that are touched in daily life; and the feelings aroused in inspections: for providers, annoyance at being checked on, feelings of inadequacy, memories of childhood; for the service users, confusion and uncertainty; for inspectors, recognising their own reactions to what they find, using their feelings to trigger thinking about the quality of life, not being overwhelmed by the sadness and despair or the joy and excitement of those who live and work in residential homes and day care.

Six

'A good enough service'

Martin Chambers and Roger Clough

THIS CHAPTER is designed to examine the ways in which an inspectorate can judge if the inspected service is 'good enough'; in addition, it provides pointers to discover whether the inspectorate is itself 'good enough', an issue which is examined further in Chapter Eight. At a time when parents were being bombarded with expert advice and were becoming anxious of the ever increasing expectations on them, Winnicott (1964) coined the phrase 'good enough parenting' both to take some of the pressure off parents but also to describe the reality: as parents we have to get a balance; we cannot achieve all that we would; time is limited; 'good enough' is what matters. So it is with the facilities subject to social services inspection.

BEING GOOD ENOUGH OR SATISFACTORY

Any inspectorate is interested in ensuring that standards of a service are satisfactory. The dilemma, of course, is the definition of 'satisfactory': the level and the components of 'being satisfactory' are not to be defined by the characteristics of an inspector's own life style. The standards of the service do not have to replicate the inspector's individual or the inspectorate's collective view of what constitutes a good life. Understandings of difference help us not to stereotype others and not to presume that what is familiar to us in our culture is the way it has to be. In this sense an inspector has to challenge assumptions and discrimination (including her or his own) to allow for proper differences. Thus, a manager's standards may be just as valid as those of the inspectorate. There is a further complexity, discussed later, as to what comprises a standard.

Within our own families and life style we select people to be with on the basis of some factors in common: shared values, interests, backgrounds, and so on. Of course, our choices do not always work out but our point is that they are choices. If we were to ask different people the question 'If you were to move into a residential home, what sort of life style would you want?' we would get hugely divergent answers. The divergence would exist whether we asked about matters connected with preferences for being with others or being separate, the arrangements for meals or the sorts of activities that were organised. There would be differences within and between managers, owners, users, relatives and inspectors.

Yet, it is the inspectorate's job to judge whether the service is 'good enough'. In one way or another the inspectorate has to manage a two fold task: to be aware of the dangers of presuming that one's own assumptions are inviolate, based as they are on one's sex, race, age, class, culture, sexual orientation, state of health and ability; but nevertheless to make a judgement as to what is and is not satisfactory. In addition, it is proper for the inspectorate to comment on ways in which a service might be improved, even though it meets the minimum requirements. One of the central factors in determining 'being satisfactory' is the service's acceptability by the user.

There is sometimes a temptation to take on trust that all is well. This is dangerous; just because an inspector is told that something is so does not mean that such is actually the case. Those being inspected have an interest in presenting their position as well as possible. As has often been remarked, 'they would say that, wouldn't they'! This chapter looks at methods which can be employed to cross check certain facts which may come to light during an inspection. An inspection unit must ensure that the service is 'good enough', and a part of that is to explore fully any areas of doubt.

Inspection is defined as 'The action of inspecting or looking narrowly into; careful scrutiny or survey; close examination' (Shorter Oxford English Dictionary). The second half of the word is derived from the Latin for 'look'; interestingly when the same Latin word is a part of speculate it is used about mentally looking at and so includes the meaning to conjecture. It is legitimate for an inspector to conjecture but the process must not stop at the stage of mentally looking at something. Nothing must be taken for granted. It must be seen with the inspector's own eyes and compared with an agreed or established standard.

It is an occupational characteristic of inspectors to be suspicious. As has been discussed in the previous chapter the stance is one of 'that's what you say but I must have my own evidence'. The important point to note here is that the inspector must develop a style of searching for, finding and cataloguing evidence.

STANDARDS AND MEASUREMENT

The distance between the monarch's imperial nose and the tips of the imperial fingers was said to be one imperial yard. There was no doubt about it. Perhaps we are more likely to trust that a metre is one hundred centimetres whether you are in Paris or Preston. Measurement must be standard in inspections as well. Once a standard has been agreed we need to be able to measure it. It is important to know that a particular inspector examining an aspect of a service in one place will apply the same standard, using the same measure as would a colleague in a different place.

Measurement requires a mechanism for measuring: for example, agreement on the standard of what constitutes a metre or a degree, and of what constitutes a ruler or a thermometer. In addition, we have to be assured that the measure is sufficiently accurate for its purpose. It is imperative that neither inspectors nor managers are in a position of discounting the information on the basis that the equipment is not reliable. It may be tempting to dismiss the evidence of bathroom scales about our own weight, but that must not happen in inspection. Indeed, one of the requirements of submission for recognition of quality assurance systems under British Standards 5750 is that there are procedures to test the reliability of equipment used in measuring. It is obvious that it is easier to devise standards and mechanisms for measuring aspects which are concrete: room size, temperature, the number of toilets, the number of staff hours which are available per resident and so on. It is very difficult to try to construct standards for taste or attitude or efficiency. We have to consider whether it is either practical or appropriate to do so.

It should be remembered that there are different means of measuring. A scale rather than a ruler is used to measure the ingredients for a cake. When making the cake it will not be improved by increasing the weight of one ingredient out of balance with the others. The significance of the analogy is that there may be relationships between factors that make up different life styles and that simply demanding the same quantity and ratio of factors in different settings is destructive. Similarly, demanding an increase in one factor out of proportion to the others, may throw the whole system into confusion. Indeed, in making the cake we may have all the right ingredients, perfectly mixed but still have to turn on the oven for the right length of time. Inspectors have to search for the subtleties of what makes up 'good enough living'.

The Social Services Inspectorate sets out three aspects of residential life which are linked to overall quality: quality of life; quality of care; quality of management (Department of

Health, 1990a). We do not want to digress into the debate on what makes up quality. However, it is useful to consider the components of two phrases which we have been using: good enough life and standards.

Gibbs and Sinclair (1992a, p.105) draw on Donabedian (1980) to pick out three major approaches to quality assessment: structure, process and outcome. This has some similarities with analyses which list inputs, conversion process and outputs, (e.g. Miller and Gwynne, 1972) though others would distinguish outcome, the end result, from output, for example the number of staff hours available per resident. Kelly and Warr (1992, pp.10-11) suggest that it is easy for inspectorates to look at inputs (for example, the numbers of staff employed), and even outputs (perhaps the numbers of people whom the staff help with bathing); what is hard is to look at outcome, the experience of a resident who has a bath. (The examples are ours, not from Kelly and Warr). Gibbs and Sinclair (1992a) emphasise the limitations of relying on assessments arising from both structure and outcome. The components of structure are the 'stable characteristics of the providers of care, the resources they have at their disposal, and the physical and organisational settings in which they work' (p.105). Donabedian suggests that these are limited because they are indirect measures of quality of care. On the other hand, Gibbs and Sinclair stress the limitations of outcome measures seen in their context as 'those aspects of a resident's well-being which can be linked directly to the care provided'. It is difficult to determine what has influenced the outcome.

Therefore, in a study to examine components of quality of life they gave special emphasis to process. The problem with these types of analyses is that while they are helpful at one level in trying to break down the task, the act of breaking down into parts destroys the whole. The reality is that for service users the outcome is a totality of factors like choice of when you want to have a bath, hot water at the right temperature and a pleasant environment and, intrinsically, the manner in which staff act towards you when they are helping you. The process of how the bathing takes place is likely to be the more important factor than many other outcome measures. In a small study in Cumbria in which residents of homes for older people were interviewed, Irving (1994) emphasised the importance of the relationship between residents and staff. 'Staff were mentioned time and time again in each interview and it is clear that staff have a major impact on quality of life' (p.50).

It is also necessary to define 'standards'. Ritchie (1992) suggests that standards serve the following functions: 'to ensure compatibility and comparability; to assure customers that the product or service is adequate for their needs; to enhance individual and organisational performance' (p.59). He argues for precision in standard setting so that the standard is measurable rather than abstract and distinguishes types of standards (ideal, exemplary, normative, ratchet and minimum) (pp.74 & 69). In addition, he shows the value of looking at the source of the standards: are they derived from existing statements (his 'eclectic' approach) or from 'constructing a hierarchy of desired outcomes or accomplishments (the 'logical' approach) (p.70)?

However the standard is drawn up, there may be circumstances where something is thought by the inspector to need change; in this case the effect of the change on the whole system must be considered. For example, if there is concern that the care is not sufficiently individualised, the introduction of a new system of record keeping is an option to be considered. The inspector and the management have to examine what will bring about the desired result – and to that end there may be more significant factors than a new record system which, without other changes, might take staff away from care of residents.

PERFORMANCE INDICATORS AND THE WHOLE PRODUCT

On occasions when caught in the administration of the detail, an inspector may forget that the purpose of the setting of a standard and of finding mechanisms is to judge the end result. The inspection is a process to enable the inspector to make a judgement, and the most significant judgement is that of the end product. In Chapter Two the situation was described of an inspector asking that an administrative system be changed because it might not be efficient if current staff were absent. That might or might not be legitimate for the inspector. The satisfactory outcome would be one where the system works well enough with existing staff and would work well enough if others had to take over. Many of the factors which are examined are best seen as performance indicators of life in that facility, whether day nursery, residential home or school. The performance indicator is an aspect being studied which is designed to provide information relevant to an understanding of a broader aspect of daily life. The significance of this analysis is that the danger is avoided of giving undue weight to the indicator and missing the view of the total product to which the indicator was intended to contribute.

Thus in considering whether a meal is good enough, various items may be considered: choice of menu, time of meal, the room where the meal takes place, the way the table has been laid and the attitude of staff. The critical factor is not whether there are three or ten choices of main course: rather, it is what the available choice (and the extent to which individuals really feel free to choose) tell the inspector about the quality of the meal.

The inspector has to use, but not rely on totally, a series of performance indicators. These performance indicators will not in themselves give a measure of the actual delivered care, nor of the attitude of those whose job it is to provide care. What they will provide is a picture which has to be interpreted.

Care planning provides an example. For the purpose of the inspection task, it is best considered as a performance indicator. Care planning is an instrument that was designed to ensure that service users were considered as individuals: what they want and need must be considered carefully (the 'assessment' stage), the options available must be considered imaginatively and realistically, planning must take place, decisions put into effect and the whole situation monitored. Within the task of care planning, it is possible to specify further indicators: is the resident consulted? are records stored in a secure area where only care staff are able to gain access? are review dates properly maintained? do people know what is being written about them? do they sign or otherwise indicate their understanding and agreement with what is recorded?

The danger of the performance indicator is that it becomes regarded as the outcome. An example of this is in the reviews carried out of young people in care. To ensure that young people and their parents were properly consulted about what was happening in their lives, detailed procedures were developed setting out, for example, the frequency of reviews, and the people who should attend. Yet, it has emerged that many young people and parents feel intimidated by the review meeting; even more significant is the fact that professionals often discuss situations before the meeting with the consequence that the effective decision making is previous to and outside the meeting (Clough, 1987, pp.41-45). Similarly it would be possible for the formality of a care planning procedure to be immaculate but for staff to be little concerned about the people who are the subjects of the plans and give little thought to what are the available options. This is the fear of all bureaucratic procedures: that the procedure may be followed and its spirit, the reason for the establishment of the procedure, may be lost.

In this, inspection is no different from other social services tasks. Child protection is an obvious example. Procedures have been developed to safeguard the welfare of children. One example must suffice: the requirement that there is consultation with key professionals before decisions are taken to amend plans. The purpose is to ensure that decisions are made with all known information available as there is abundant evidence of the mistakes that are made when one worker pursues an individual line. Staff, not understanding or not accepting of the need for consultation, may see the requirement as unnecessarily formal. The parallel for inspectors is to understand the reasons for the procedure or use of a performance indicator. The task is not to impose a particular type of care plan: rather it is to find a way of assessing whether or not people are treated as individuals with proper consideration of their needs, proper planning and proper implementation.

In addition to the 'I do believe you but I must see for myself' approach, inspectors must also attain a 'So it's not how I would have done it, but does it work?' way of looking at things. It is very easy to be closed to alternative systems and styles: the fact that practice does not conform to a predetermined standard does not mean it is not satisfactory. It may be different and better than the inspectorate's ideas of quality; or it may be different and worse but still of a good enough standard.

In searching for the particular, it is possible to lose the totality. Assessments of quality can be a trade off: one thing superb, far better than the inspectorate could have hoped to expect, another not as good as it should be. Sometimes the detail of the inspectorate's wishes or requirements may work against the overall objectives. The creation of a homely and domestic atmosphere, valued by many service users, may be put in jeopardy by the formality and detail of care planning procedures, fire precaution work or even scrupulous adherence to Food Act Regulations. Our definition of 'good enough' is not the same as 'minimum'. 'Good enough' is an overall judgement. Thus an inspector may judge that, in the circumstances and the context in which an establishment operates, many aspects were good, others not so good and perhaps one or two fairly poor: overall, the conclusion may be that this was 'good enough'.

The purpose of inspection is to protect vulnerable people and to foster as good a life style for individuals as possible. If any aspect of inspection does not work towards or achieve this purpose, then it should be dropped. Inspectors are not themselves providing residential services to vulnerable people. They are registering, monitoring and inspecting the services which are provided by other people. Where possible, the staff providing the service should be left to get on with their task.

Underlying any regulatory activity are questions as to its necessity, its procedures and its outcome. In Chapter Two the issue was raised in relation to independent boarding schools of whether parents are sufficiently protected by the fact of choosing to buy a service that they do not need to purchase. The standard argument of the providers in these circumstances is that it is in their own interests to make sure that the quality is high: they are selling a service just like any other business and if customers do not wish to buy it then they can go elsewhere. Yet there is virtually no current argument for total deregulation. As has been shown, when the Government dipped its toe into the deregulation water (Department of Health, 1993c) there was minimal support: most providers argued that they needed regulation so that the public would be assured of the quality of their products on the basis that bad providers would be weeded out. It is accepted that in certain respects consumers of any service or product need protection, whether in relation to health and safety or the quality of the product. The debate focuses on which aspects should be the subject of regulation and what should be the mechanisms.

In relation to the facilities which are the subject of this book, the regulation issue hinges on the capacity of people to make informed choices and the degree of risk if the service is inadequate. The relevance for this chapter is the extent to which regulation should intrude into the daily life of users. For example, some managers argue that it is unnecessary or patronising for inspectorates to insist on a high ratio of single to double rooms. Their argument is that some people want to share. The inspector is aware of other dimensions, in particular that it is very hard to ensure that the resident is free to choose. Alongside a formal system, there are strong informal pressures from managers to which residents are vulnerable. In these circumstances, the inspectorate may acknowledge the manager's point that not all residents want a single room but hold to a stringent requirement for all new rooms to be single and for there to be a high ratio of single to double rooms for existing rooms.

The justification is three fold: first, the buildings may be in existence for many years and, on current trends, there will be greater demand for single rooms as housing standards rise for space and privacy; secondly, individuals who wish to share can do so by having adjoining rooms; thirdly, the only way to ensure that people really are able to choose is to have the option of single or shared accommodation available. Inspection units have to examine their standards in this sort of way to know whose interests they are promoting when they argue for specific standards.

The same point holds for the detail of standards. When measuring anything to do with a residential home, school or day nursery, there are different potential starting points: the point of view of the user, the relative, the home owner, the staff member, the inspector, the councillor and the amorphous public. There is always a danger than an inspector will assume that his/her own personal standards are 'right' or 'normal'. To measure something and to compare it with a normal, domestic standard depends on an individual perception of what constitutes 'normal' or 'domestic'. For example, is it to be expected that a tea tray will be set with or without a cloth? In fact in the 1990s is it even normal to have a tea tray at all? Should a cup of tea be offered without biscuits or a milk bottle be put on the table? Is it 'domestic' to have walls painted with emulsion paint, or to have fancy knickknacks all over the place? Many residents might disagree with an inspectorate's statement that they should be permitted to stop in bed all morning; the notion of not getting up is alien to their culture. Similarly, a resident may feel that it is normal to be expected to carry out tasks within the residential home, since it is their home.

Further, it is imperative to remember that a residential

home is not the same as an individual's own home: residents are living alongside people with whom they have not chosen to live, they are confronted by the living styles of different people, the numbers of people in one building are greater than in one's own home and the people providing the care are not doing so just for oneself or one's family, as they would be if they were coming in to clean or cook in one's own house. In fact, the nature of the household is different. The point is stressed because there are powerful consequent reasons for some standards in a residential home being different from those in an ordinary household.

The case being put is not that each detail has to be agreed by everybody; that would be a recipe for inaction. Nor is the view of users automatically to be accepted. Individual service users may be as inappropriately prescriptive of the way a place should run as anyone else, knowing what they think to be best for others. Rather, the point being made is that in reaching its decision the inspectorate must consider the perspectives of the different stakeholders. It may then be proper for an inspectorate to set a standard that as part of their daily routine residents are to be able to get up when they wish even though for most residents that may be an irrelevance. Whether or not this becomes written as a standard will depend on the extent to which the inspectorate judges this as an important aspect of daily life for those who do wish to stay in bed. What is to be avoided is inspectorates assuming that they know what other people want. There is little point in setting standards without knowing whether or not they are thought reasonable by users or providers, let alone other stakeholders.

Thus, decisions have to be made as to the aspects of daily life on which inspectorates should comment. Some of these judgements will be more contentious than others. Two examples from childminder provision are whether dogs should be allowed to exercise in areas where children will play and whether childminders should be allowed to smoke. Should the view of a parent that she/he has no objection to either of these make any difference? There remains the inevitability that inspectorates at times will focus on different things than users. Sometimes residents may think the item to be less important than does the inspector: 'Inspectors should focus on our rights and not on our menus'; at others the requirements of inspectors seem patronising: 'We feel that there is no need for a daily register in everyday life ... we are not children and we would like you to take this into consideration please' (Cumbria County Council, 1994, pp.5 & 2).

In any case there will be some factors which the inspectorate will decide not to examine either because they are thought less significant or because they lie within the domain of provider/user negotiation. A resident might have a private phone and make arrangements with the manager for payment; an inspector might intervene only in circumstances where the resident is complaining about the arrangement. The same might be true about value for money: the starting position for the inspector is to check whether someone is getting the service specified in the contract, not whether the resident has chosen to pay more than the inspector thinks the service is worth. An inspector's core task is not to look at value for money for the resident, that is the job of the resident or the resident's family. There are provisos which would come into effect if it appeared that the resident was being hood winked or was not able to make such a judgement.

Inspectorates should judge against a predetermined, minimum standard. We have stressed that the core regulatory activity is determining whether or not a facility reaches what has been set as the standard that is the minimum acceptable. There are two reasons for stressing this: the first is that there is a temptation for inspectors to want to be involved in activities which may seem the more exciting, worthwhile or are at least less judgmental; secondly, managers must be clear as to whether the comments being made are suggestions or requirements. That is not to deny that an inspection unit may have a legitimate interest in development above that minimum level.

TRYING TO UNCOVER WHETHER THE SERVICE IS GOOD ENOUGH

It is not just the care home which must be good enough, so must the inspectorate and the inspector. There must be techniques available to the inspectors to ensure that they are not too keen to trust what they are told, nor too ready to dismiss. 'The truth is', as Oscar Wilde wrote in *The Importance of being Ernest* 'rarely pure and never simple. Modern life would be very tedious if it were either'. Truth is sometimes difficult to uncover and it is often the case that conditions will combine to fool people into thinking they have witnessed something they have not. Such factors may be presented deliberately to create a particular desired effect as Paul Daniels has been doing to make a living for many years.

If we take as a hypothesis that most managers are not dishonest, nevertheless we have to accept being honest does not mean that people will not try to present themselves in the best possible light. We all present ourselves to the outside world, an activity to which Goffman (1956) drew attention in his book *Presentation of Self in Everyday Life*. At an inspection we are likely to take particular care as to how we present ourselves. It is difficult to determine when presentation becomes deviousness and when that in turn merges into deceit. Fortunately, inspectors do not have to determine motivation: they have to find ways to study what is happening in order to be in a position to judge the quality of the provision. The skill lies in knowing how to accomplish that.

There is sometimes a danger of asking a question and assuming you can see the whole picture. There used to be an advertisement on television for a particular newspaper where a scene was shot from several different angles, each one shown in turn. Only the last shot enabled you to see what was really happening. Take for example a simple question, 'Are residents able to use their bedroom whenever they wish?'. The answer could well be 'Yes', and be recorded as such. Was that the answer the inspector wanted? Perhaps, but was it the right question?

Supplementary questions which may result in a clearer

picture could be: 'Are residents able to get to their rooms whenever they wish?' 'Are rooms heated to an acceptable temperature throughout a twenty four hour period?' 'Is there a comfortable chair, and access to a radio, television, telephone?' 'Can residents have their meals in their room?' 'Is there a culture within the home which encourages residents to use their room?' The list of questions is only restricted by the imagination of the inspector.

Similarly, an inspector may ask the proprietor for a medical record of a resident for June and be given a medical record for June. She/he may assume that it is the June of the current year but that may not be the case! If the inspector asks to see the care record for a particular resident and is told 'You would pick that one, she is no longer a resident here!', a gullible inspector might just leave well alone and think that such was the case. A better response is, 'That's all right, let me see the record any way'. After all the home is required to hold on to the record for a minimum of three years (Regulation 6.4) and that record should show the date the resident left the home, transferred to hospital or died (Regulation 6.1.2) (Residential Care Homes Regulations, 1984).

There are limitations to the usefulness of records as a means of uncovering the real life of the home. Anyone can construct a sentence which implies the opposite from what is actually written. Words like 'perhaps', 'apparent' or 'seemed' can be dropped into sentences to take the edge off a statement. Sentences can be constructed to mislead on purpose. Events can occur which go unrecorded. The fact that something has not been recorded does not mean that the event did not occur.

Similarly, statements in brochures may not be accurate. What is written may mean something quite different to one person than another. What for example is the difference between the words 'alternative' and 'choice'?

The task for inspectorate staff is to use both the statement and the absence of a statement to examine the life of the establishment. Thus, an inspector may want to check when residents get up. There are a variety of options: look at the brochure; ask different staff; look at staff rotas; check any Notes of Guidance for Staff; ask different residents; observe on unannounced visits; study records to see which staff get residents up and when they are on duty. In carrying out the search, the skills referred to earlier have to put into effect. In many circumstances it is better to ask people open than closed questions: 'Tell me about the start of your day', rather than 'What time do you get up?' Material has to be cross checked: if the night staff are expected to help the residents to get up for breakfast, then it should be possible to work back from the breakfast time to the sort of time that the first residents are got up. Having exposed the fact that a statement which claims that residents get up in time for breakfast at eight o'clock is misleading since several residents are being dressed at 6 o'clock, the answer may be that the early rise is only for the residents who want to get up at that time because they have been awake all night. There are further questions for the inspector to pursue.

A manager who says on an inspection visit, 'Look at this!' may in fact be saying, 'Don't look at that!'. Behind the comment 'We are having a trip this afternoon' may have been the realisation that at the last inspection residents had said they were bored, that the manager had suggested taking them out more and had not done it. Residents can be prompted to say the right things; the residents who will say what are thought by staff to be helpful things can happen to be around, witness the manager's comment in Chapter Two. District nurses can by invitation appear on the scene just after the inspector arrives.

Records which are apparently in order and up to date can often tell the observer more than the manager expects. A fire drill which happened the week before an announced inspection might indicate that reasonable fire precautions are being adopted. It could also indicate that things are being brought up to date to impress the inspector.

More overt stage dressing is demonstrated by staff styles of approach to residents, perhaps hugging and kissing a resident to demonstrate how well he/she gets on with the residents. The task for the inspector is to determine whether the behaviour is typical and whether it is acceptable.

The activities which hold the key to inspection may be those things which the staff member may not be aware of doing. These can be good or bad. They may be almost imperceptible. A member of staff is heard asking a resident if he/she wants to go to the toilet, saying to another care assistant 'Mr or Mrs XXX is wet again'. Or someone tries to show the inspector into a resident's room without knocking or asking permission. Someone else may discuss a particular resident with the inspector within the hearing of the resident (Clough, 1981, p.160). A comment made as an aside by a resident will often tell the inspector more about the home than the most detailed records. 'I have told them I don't like sprouts' gives the lie to the well presented menu offering a full choice.

Tunnel vision during an inspection is to be avoided. An over concentration on predetermined goals has the effect of obscuring other matters which might come to light given half the chance. The inspector must aim both to focus on particular issues but to stay alive to what is happening. Beedell (1983) refers to 'using radar' to describe the skill of residential workers who need to give attention to what they are doing but at the same time to be aware of all that is going on around them, for example noting the fact that the volume has risen sharply at the end of the building or that there is a sudden silence. Inspectors need the same skills.

RETURNING TO THE DEFINITION OF GOOD ENOUGH

One of the problems with words is that they mean differing things to different people. Hermann Hess once stated: 'Words are really a mask. They rarely express the true meaning; in fact they tend to hide it' (Serranc, 1966).

Inspection reports must be as clear and precise as possible. In the reports inspectorate staff set out to inform others of the quality of provision in a particular place. When someone sits down to write any report, he/she is using words to convey a judgement. We know that the desired objective is influenced by what is written. People present information about individuals in various types of reports: about themselves in application forms; about others in references or court reports. Probably we have learnt that what is not stated may be as significant as what is written. How many employers have been willing to hide their real judgements in order to get rid of someone! A dangerous game! The inspection report, written to a pre-set structure, must avoid that. Somehow, inspectorates have to work out their view on an establishment and present that clearly. The language used is of immense significance.

If we acknowledge the ambivalence in the feelings of managers and other staff to inspections, we recognise that although people rationally may want criticism, they also want praise and confirmation of their activity. Whatever the structure of an inspection report, relying on check lists or written statements, it is important that the judgement of the inspectorate about the quality of the service is apparent. There is the world of difference between a place that is satisfactory and one that is outstanding. Properly, managers are very upset when the good aspects of their care are glossed over.

The inspection report is a particular and an unusual type of feedback in that it is both for the provider of the service and for the public. Nevertheless, the usual maxims for giving feedback are helpful: do not make general statements, in particular about inadequacy; be specific; provide evidence; write statements in ways which suggest how improvements may be made.

To be able to demonstrate differences in quality, the inspectorate has to consider its use of language. What is meant by 'unsatisfactory', 'acceptable', 'satisfactory', 'good', 'first class' or 'excellent'? The task becomes one of defining the words and thinking of how judgements are to be made. Different approaches, of course, may be equally valid. Thus, one inspectorate may only use two categories 'unsatisfactory' and 'satisfactory'; another may aim to distinguish different aspects of provision on some sort of scale. If the first approach is adopted, it is important that the text of the report demonstrates the substantial differences that there may be between two satisfactory establishments.

Another aspect of 'defining good enough' in reports is to match requirements and recommendations with the judgement of the report. Again language has immense significance. The two examples which follow of the summary of a report illustrate the difference:

> a) '**Conclusion** ... This establishment has achieved a good standard in all aspects inspected. Some possibilities to consider for future developments are...'.

> b) '**Conclusion** ... Satisfactory. The following recommendations are made...'.

The format of the report ought to encourage the inspector to reach a judgement about the overall quality of the establishment and about individual aspects within that, not to prevent that from happening.

In making recommendations, it is imperative that the inspector should not demand anything from a manager without being clear what is wanted. An example of this can be found in Conduct of the Home (Regulation 9.2) requiring that there is a system to 'ascertain the wishes and feelings of the residents'. So, if there is a statement in a report that the establishment does not have an adequate system in place to find out the views of residents, it is then incumbent on the inspector to be able to quote chapter and verse on what is an adequate system, and to be able to provide guidance as to how such a desirable state can be achieved (Residential Care Homes Regulations, 1984).

The requirements and recommendations made in the inspection report must take account of the nature of the problem; to do that they must include an assessment of risk, of urgency and of a realistic time scale for introducing the change. For example, it would not be reasonable for an inspection report to demand that within a period of one month a new laundry system should be provided within the home. Nor should any vague recommendations be made such as 'improving care planning' without first providing a definition of what is required.

CONCLUSION

The Registered Homes Act 1984 and the Children Act 1989 place an obligation on inspectorates to inspect. It places no obligation on home owners and managers to like being inspected. But if the inspectorate demands high standards from the places it inspects, then those establishments should be able to demand equally high standards from the inspectorate.

Seven

Putting inspections into effect

Roger Clough

Roger Clough

INTRODUCTION

THIS CHAPTER, which might have been entitled 'Getting the show on the road', focuses on the mechanics: the procedures and systems which will help to ensure that the primary task of the organisation is achieved. In many ways 'the mechanics' appear mundane and uninteresting: inspection visits and making judgements seem the more vital parts of the work. Indeed, systems may be thought to get in the way of the real work. For many, the notion of systems creates instant recollections of demands for keeping files and records in ways that make it more difficult to give time and attention to what really matters. This idea of systems as being unproductive for the task of the organisation is a constant theme in any job and there seems little likelihood that the computer, with its potential to store still more data, will change attitudes or requirements.

I am aware that I have left writing this chapter until towards the end of this book, in part because other aspects of inspection seemed more interesting. What is to be said about systems? are they something to get excited about? will new revelations and understandings be found here? Yet, I know the energy I put into working with others in Cumbria to develop systems for inspection. I have no doubt that they are integral to the production of good services. If one reason for the reluctance to write about systems is that it is hard to make the topic come alive, another is that systems at times are antagonistic to the core activity of the organisation. There is a tendency for them to take on a life of their own. Any bureaucratic process (and the word 'bureaucratic' is used here in a neutral, descriptive sense) may become an end in itself. This is not a new realisation: Dickens and Camus are amongst a myriad of writers who have exposed the problem.

It is here that the core of the dilemma is to be found: good intent has to be transformed into good practice. To achieve that we have to think about the process of that transformation, and then establish structures and systems which will produce the desired result. I am using the word 'systems' as shorthand for the means within the organisation of producing the end product: the collection of procedures, filing and record systems, monitoring arrangements and internal regulations. Processes and systems for putting inspections into effect have to be placed at the top of the agenda precisely because what is wanted is systems that will help achieve the primary task, and what is not wanted is systems that will impede that task. In any organisation a key question about performance is whether systems promote the core activity.

Systems are mundane but the quality of inspection performance will be found in mundane activities such as whether people are listened to, letters answered or reports produced on time; the mundane is important because it is the staple, but it does not have to be dull.

Systems, I stressed at the start of this chapter, are means to an end: they do not make the judgement, review the options or take action, However, they are the mechanism by which evidence about a particular establishment is clearly recorded, or information is made available to everybody as to the standards for registration and the powers of the inspectorate. A part of what is required from systems is that they provide the information that is wanted for the task.

In some ways the essence of the work appears deceptively simple, the design of procedures to achieve the primary task. This would suggest a logical process: establish the primary task, decide the means by which that task is best undertaken, put them into effect. Two critical factors come into play. The first is that the system must allow for the change and struggle that is an inevitable part of putting dreams and objectives into practice: good practice emerges as inspectors realise the inappropriateness of what they are doing at present and search for better ways. Secondly, systems are not exclusive to sections of organisations: the inspectorate has to create systems which will mesh with those of the wider organisation as well as being the most suitable for its own work.

SYSTEMS FOR OBJECTIVES

As in any other welfare activity, inspectors have to determine both what they are in the business of doing and the systems that will produce the desired objectives. Thus, we move into the world of mission statements and business plans. For some, these are anathema, signalling the inappropriate advance of the business world into social service activity; others view them with cynicism; a third group, of which I am a part, would use such language and systems provided that they are used to drive the service in the direction that is wanted. The use of mission statements as part of a demonstration of commitment and establishment of quality is discussed in Kelly and Warr (1992, pp.5 – 9). Whatever language is used, organisations should review their work, looking at the demands, the boundaries and limits to their activities; then they should set out their objectives, the means by which they will achieve them and the systems that will monitor progress. It is probable that such plans will include measures of performance and specify the training and support that is available for staff.

I regard the fundamental issue to be that of determining the primary task of the inspectorate, the overriding purpose including the value base. In any organisation individual workers make decisions as to what they should do in certain circumstances. The raison d'être of a mission statement is not that it tells people what will happen in specific circumstances; rather, it is that by setting out the nature of the task and the inherent values, individuals may determine the action they will take. A similar issue underlies the use of particular systems: no system provides the right answers nor creates the right climate for work. Yet, if the nature of the task is understood, systems have to be in place to ensure that the task can be delivered. The system has to be secondary to the task.

Current debates about quality assurance and British Standards illustrate this. Indeed, it is not surprising that the phrase quality babble has been introduced! Many people would accept that the word quality has become so over used that it is in danger of becoming meaningless. Whatever system is in place, there is potential for the process of the system to appear to be managed competently, yet for the purpose to be lost for which the system exists: thus, files may be kept up to date but the judgements in them be poor; business plans be produced with irrelevant targets, or procedures be written and followed, but the service remain unchanged. To gain credits in a charter systems I must answer letters on time, seemingly without regard to the content of the response. The fault for this lies not in the system but in the implementation of the system; the system always should be subsidiary to the purpose of the organisation or task.

In this chapter I do not argue the case for particular processes or systems, though I use specific examples as illustration. However, I set out the case in inspection for effectiveness (in terms of sound judgement, consistency and a willingness to act when appropriate) and efficiency (using resources to best effect). As in residential work, it is in the detail that it becomes apparent whether the grand aims are realised. Systems and processes matter because they are the means by which the objective is translated into action or the means by which the translation of the objective into action is thwarted. Burton, (1993) writing about residential work, has three chapter headings which touch on the essentials: Creating helpful organisation, Resisting hindering organisation and Liberating institutions.

These headings highlight the need to create an organisation which will facilitate the achievement of the primary task, and free people to do their job. Examples from occasions when social service work is placed under intense scrutiny illustrate the issue. Investigations, most frequently those in child protection, arouse vast anxieties about the adequacy of the work of the organisation. It seems to many people that the purpose of the procedures for child protection work is to ensure that no blame may be attributed to the social services department, in particular its senior management. In other words the procedures are taken to be of value in defensive terms, to demonstrate that staff carried out their work to the letter of what was specified. By contrast to that perception, the good procedure is the one that is produced to enhance the carrying out of the task. In fact many of the child protection procedures have been developed in precisely that way; they have been established to promote co-operative work between agencies in which information is shared and differences in opinion are examined. Yet, too often, staff remain unconvinced. How has this come about?

Partly, staff have not been involved sufficiently in setting the procedures; partly, they find the reality of their day to day work to be that managers are not available sufficiently for support and consultation; partly the mechanics that were designed, for example, to ensure co-operation have become rigid and result in the designated review meetings being called but there being no real debate in the meetings. The lessons are apparent: staff must be involved in system design; the procedures must lead to support for the core activity and they must be used with imagination in line with the reason for which they were introduced.

The importance of systems must be stressed. They do not dispense with personal and structural issues. Nevertheless, they are essential in ensuring that the task is carried out. Thus, the key to successful practice in this regard lies in understanding the significance and subtlety of an issue and in producing a system which will enhance the ability of the organisation to deliver what is wanted. Without systems, our insights and intentions result in haphazard implementation. With inappropriate systems, these same insights and intentions are lost or distorted. The trick is to keep testing task against system and system against task. In this way systems are not viewed as absolutes but as mechanisms. A system appropriate for the task at any one time may be dispensed with when something else becomes of greater significance.

This approach is one way to examine the certainty, sometimes indeed the arrogance, of much writing on management. An example follows: some people advocate the scrapping of records of certain meetings because in that way people will listen carefully, will check on their commitments, will not be overwhelmed by paper and will become aware of their loyalty to the group. Indeed, the same is sometimes argued for residential homes. Yet as a general truth for management it would be a disaster. The system has to match the task, which must take account of the stage of individuals and groups (Brown and Clough, 1989, pp.39-40). There is no single system which should be adopted, nor any particular technique which will produce the magic of quality.

In a way, the result that is wanted is the same as that stressed throughout this book in relation to performance indicator on the one hand, and overall judgement on the other. The performance indicator is not an end in itself; it provides a clue to reaching a judgement. In the same way the system is to be judged by the extent to which it creates the desired outcome, not by whether it is efficiently managed.

THEMES AND ATTRIBUTES OF INSPECTION

It is tempting to set out certain attributes as if they are stages in inspections or the life of inspectorates. The reality is that although some factors are more likely to occur in an early or late stage, they recur at any time. It is a little like Erikson (1950) writing of critical stages of human life which are associated with particular times in the life cycle: but the issues that were in need of resolution at any one time may present themselves again. Thus, the stages are both events and processes.

The primary task

Inspection is an art in that it requires imagination, creativity and spontaneity. Inspectors have to search for answers to questions like: What is it like to be here? How do users feel? At times a leap towards understanding or towards finding out is wanted. Yet, inspection also is a science in terms of other necessary factors: method, discipline and checks. Clues come from various sources and senses; inspectors must be open to such clues. Indeed, investigation reports sometimes highlight the clues that were available and not recognised or acted on at the time. Thus inspectors have to search for clues and contrary instances; they must take little or nothing on trust. The task is to reach a judgement and in doing so to use performance indicators not as ends in themselves but as mechanisms to provide evidence for the overarching factor that is being considered. At issue, for example, is not so much the extent of choice for users (though that has some significance) but whether users feel able to express their views and make use of the choice that is said to exist. Beyond that, we have to know how significant is choice as part of a total understanding of quality of life.

The inspector must have a passion for people's welfare, knowledge, a willingness to risk judgements, persistence, an ability to exercise authority in a satisfactory way and a capacity to be open to the pain and hurt of others. The knowledge required includes an understanding of good and bad practice in residential and day care, of people in their environment (development, psychology, sociology, social policy and some medical background) and of legislation and procedures.

Thus, individual inspectors face issues and dilemmas:

1. they have to be themselves and yet consistent with the core values, standards and procedures of the inspectorate;
2. they are to be independent minded, driving an inspectorate agenda and at the same time co-operating with providers, users, councillors and managers;
3. they must find a way to carry out a repetitive task and keep fresh and alert;
4. they have to live with an expectation that they will act with integrity, at times as if they were the sole repository of the conscience of the organisation;
5. they have to 'present' themselves and in this sense an inspection can be seen as a performance;
6. their task is not casual: there is planning, preparation and rehearsal; it is as if a script was prepared with a recognition that it may be necessary to move from it;
7. their work is semi public: it is in part observed by various stakeholders who have an interest in its outcome; as such it is open to observation and question.

At the heart of what is needed is an ability and a willingness to make judgements, knowing that their own actions will be held up to scrutiny.

The systems and procedures that I shall discuss in the rest of this chapter must be used to create the type of environment and the type of inspection practice that are wanted.

Consultation

Inspectorates have to discuss the inspection system with a number of interested parties, to listen to what is said and then to work out their own position. It is imperative that the nature of power is specified. There is a temptation to talk of 'co-operation' and 'partnership' without clarifying limitations. Inspectors should try to work with customers in as co-operative style as possible, but the diverse interest groups are not equal partners; inspectors, properly, retain the responsibility for many decisions and much damage is done by not explaining this to people from the start. This fact leaves the inspectorate open to the charge that any consultation is cosmetic: 'After all', it may be argued, 'we said what we thought should happen and you have taken no notice'. The task for inspectorates therefore is to find a system which will give them maximum opportunity to listen, to discuss and consider the points put to them, and to explain the reasons for decisions that are made.

In Chapter Three Albert Cook and Eileen Gentry emphasised the value of an inspector visiting a home before an inspection so that all parties have an opportunity to get to know the parameters and expectations of the forthcoming inspection. On a wider scale, the same is true of the unit as a whole: there are immense advantages in finding time and procedures to discuss the functioning of the unit with those who are interested. As with other systems for consultation, there are immediate questions about whether proceedings should be informal or formal, and whether consultation should be with individuals who are representatives of organisations, and perhaps mandated by them. No system provides all the answers, so the task is to produce a system (in the sense of a package of procedures) which will allow the best opportunity for achieving objectives.

It is probable that the more in harmony are the expectations of inspections of all groups, the greater will be the success of inspection. Millham, Bullock and Cherrett (1975, pp.45-72) examine the extent to which different types of goals within approved schools (instrumental, expressive and organisational) were valued by differing groups of people, in particular staff and boys. It is probable that approved schools were more successful when the expectations of these different groups (and of parents) were compatible. However, the knowledge that agreement on goals and procedures improves prospects for development of services must not lead inspectorates to a position where they rate so highly the potential consequences of harmony that they lose their core responsibility for decision making. Such decision making in any case does not rest solely with the inspection unit: inspectorates have responsibility under the authority of management and councillors.

One problem for the inspectorate is that of multiple systems for consultation. There is a requirement placed on inspectorates that there are consultation procedures which involve managers, users, councillors and people from other interest groups. It is useful to add staff and relatives to such meetings. If these meetings do not provide an adequate forum with a wide exchange of views, other types of meetings may be necessary. The position is complicated by the fact that while it would be comparatively easy to give representation to associations of playgroups or home owners, it is far harder to ensure that there is opportunity for people who do not belong to such groups to have their views represented. There may be elements of formal procedures at these meetings which are intimidating for some people who attend; forms of training or support are valuable if the presence of users is to be more than token. It is important also that there is clarity about both the status of the meetings (including authority for any decisions) and about the ways in which the views from consultative meetings are fed into other decision making structures. Those with an interest in proceedings who are not members of the meeting need a means of placing items on the agenda and of getting feedback from meetings.

Inspection units must get to know the views of those who are their 'customers', and they must discuss and explain their decisions. The word 'customer' allows an interesting discussion of who are the customers of inspectorates and of which groups of people should be consulted. There may be a tendency to focus on consultation with users and managers, and to neglect other professionals and councillors. In a field like that of regulation, rumour is likely to be rife and good information is paramount. If it is correct, as suggested earlier, that the more congruity there is between views of inspectors and others, then this process of consultation is critical. Inspectorate staff need knowledge (for example of the structures in their authority) but also require skills in communication. The willingness of inspectorate staff to search for solutions to the problems of customers is an important component of successful practice.

The implementation of satisfactory consultation is far harder than writing the words: inspectorates, under authority, consult with customers; they determine what they wish to take forward, whether in the consultative meeting or with papers to decision making meetings; they explain reasons for not taking forward other items or for taking them forward with a view to rejection; they take issues for decision to the appropriate decision making body.

Consistency

Managers have to ensure both that individual inspectors are consistent in their approach to different establishments and that the team of inspectors is consistent. This is common to many other jobs: both an individual teacher and a group of teachers have to be consistent in marking work, in particular when there are critical events such as exams and award of certificates; thus there develop marking criteria, marking frameworks and moderation. The inspectorate management has to establish agreement amongst staff on the standards (and how they are interpreted) and the process (the way in which individuals work and implement the systems). The system has to be demonstrably fair (even-handed) between individual facilities and between sectors.

In Cumbria there was an attempt to ensure equivalence in the ways in which independent sector and local authority homes were treated in spite of the legislative difference (Cumbria County Council, 1993b). On the initiatives of councillors and officers procedures were established which as nearly as possible were equivalent in both sectors. In brief this laid down a system to which the authority voluntarily committed itself:

1. The same words, 'Recommendations' and 'Requirements', would be used in reports on independent and local authority homes to specify degree of seriousness of finding.
2. When requirements were imposed on any home the inspectorate, first, would attempt to get agreement from the manager on action to be taken and time-scale.
3. If this proved impossible, the manager would have the right of discussing with inspectorate management and then of an appeal to a Social Services Sub Committee.
4. The manager of an independent home would have the right of appeal to Registered Homes Tribunal.
5. If the manager's position was not upheld at appeal, the inspectorate would take action against the manager by proposing to cancel registration, requiring compliance or by informing the Director, Chair of Social Services Committee and committee spokespersons that immediate action was required.
6. If there were judged to be immediate danger to residents then with an independent sector home the Inspectorate would apply to a Justice of the Peace for an order to cancel registration or vary conditions and with a local authority home would recommend to Chair and Spokespersons of Committee that immediate action should be taken to remove residents to ensure their safety.

Working with others

The theme, working with others, encompasses both this work with interested parties and more formal relationships with other agencies. There are requirements to work with a wide range of staff, including planning, environmental health and fire services. Inspectorates would do well to be clear as to the areas in which they are taking advice from others and those in which other authorities have decision making responsibility. The temptation to avoid exposing differences between professions, and so to compromise, may be particularly powerful if both groups of officers work for the same authority. Two examples will set the scene. First is a situation where the inspectorate and the fire service are reviewing or determining standards for a facility (perhaps a child minder, three bedded home or small group home). The focus of the fire service is safety; in these circumstances it is possible that it may wish to impose more stringent standards than does the inspectorate, which takes account of arrangements for daily living. There is a proper tension here which should be discussed and resolved, involving users and managers if possible. However, the authority for this particular decision does not rest with the fire service: the fire service is providing advice for the inspectorate which does not have to accept the advice given. There are other occasions when the fire service has full (and independent) authority, for example to seek an injunction to close down an establishment if it judges there to be immediate and life threatening risks. To return to the situation where an inspectorate does not wish to accept the advice of the fire service: the implications of rejecting such advice are serious and the inspection unit may decide to inform the Director or more probably a Committee of councillors of the disagreement so that a decision is made in full knowledge of the divergent advice.

A second example concerns safety standards for hot water systems in relation to legionella. Advice from within the authority (for example, from health and safety or buildings sections) will specify the safest system to ensure that there is minimal danger from legionella. The inspectorate has to determine whether or not to take that advice. In reaching its decision it has to decide on the degree of risk from legionella and place that alongside other risks in day care facilities and residential homes and schools. There is a vital principle at stake: the responsibility and authority of the inspectorate to decide specific matters in the context of its overall knowledge. Thus, the risk of a legionella outbreak is minimal even for those with the highest risks, such as older people in residential homes. I know of no case of legionella in a residential home. On the other hand risks from scalding, fire and electrical fault are far greater.

It would be a mistake for the inspectorate, in taking the advice about the safest system to eliminate risks from legionella, to require systems be put in place which would set back work on the more urgent problems. Indeed, even if any particular review of standards does not have to be set against other work of higher priority, the inspection unit must balance the minimising of risk with the consequences of so doing. Given the minimal risk from legionella to residents of a home for older people, the safest system for reducing risk from legionella may not be worth the cost. In other circumstance the reduction of risk may lead to unacceptable results: twenty years ago some of the heavy fire doors in residential homes had the effect of stopping some residents moving around buildings: was the risk worth the result?

Health and social services inspectorates
Liaison with health authorities is of particular significance. First, many residential homes for adults are dually registered with both local authority and health authority; secondly, there is the potential for managers and owners of residential homes for adults to switch registration from one authority to the other. Guidance notes have stressed the importance of both authorities considering their working relationship.

As mentioned earlier, in some areas joint units of health and social services staff have been established. This is one system designed to lead to better working relationships. However, as has been stressed at the start of this chapter, no system on its own solves problems so no system ensures standardisation or co-operation or, indeed, appropriate difference. The issues that the two authorities have to resolve are:

1. the extent to which they will adopt common standards for registration and inspection; there must be a measure of difference related to specific tasks, such as the requirement that nurses be available in a nursing home;
2. the extent to which they will adopt common procedures for registration and inspection, in particular related to: procedures at registration; the frequency of inspection

visits; the style of reports and feedback to owners and managers; the availability of reports and other information to the public; the procedure for taking action when judged necessary;

3. the ways by which they will share their individual views of residential homes, question each other's perspective and judgement and by which they will reach common or distinct conclusions both as to the quality of provision and any action required by inspectorates;

4. whether they will try to ensure equivalent styles of management, for example in relation to supervision and training of inspectorate staff;

5. the way in which reports will be presented to owners and managers, their own line managers, to councillors or health authorities and to the public;

6. definitions, in particular of:
   a) what comprises the distinction between residential and nursing care,
   b) when someone in a residential bed who is getting additional community nursing has to be reclassified as a nursing home resident *and*
   c) the various categories of provision (for example, people with mental illness).

Joint units have worked out different ways of managing staff, determining the pay and conditions of service of staff and of specifying authority for action. They also have to take account of the fact that nearly always the social services inspection unit will be far larger than that of the health authority as there are far more facilities for the local authority unit to inspect. This could lead to health authority units feeling that they are being swallowed up by the social service unit. In addition, there is the dilemma for the local authority unit that closer working relationship with the health authority in relation to residential homes for adults may lead to a split or distance from registration and inspection of children's services within their own authority. There are substantial gains for local authority inspectorates in combining the management of the registration and inspection of adults and children's services and, therefore, there are dangers of this being lost.

A precise example illustrates a wider theme. Individual inspectors from either authority will form views about the quality of provision in a home. Insofar as these are produced in reports which are publicly available there are no problems in information being shared. However, if inspectors have opinions which they are checking or allegations which they are pursuing, at what stage should these be shared with another authority? The complexity and dilemma are not done away with by neat, administrative systems. Whatever procedure is adopted owners and managers must be informed of its existence. There are pitfalls in both early and easy sharing of information and in little shared knowledge. On the one hand, there is a danger of collusion, with individuals not first working out their own perspective before agreeing a course of action; and, on the same tack, there is potential to let one authority act on your behalf because it is easier to sit back and let them get involved in the dirty work of taking action about a problem. On the other hand, there is the nonsensical position of one authority having significant concerns which they fail to share with the other.

What emerges from this discussion are general points about partnership and liaison: that co-operation takes time and energy; that closer working relationships with one group may lead to less close relationships with another; that combining previously separate units does not on its own dispense with former issues about authority and decision making and the management of different perspectives. Power, especially its location and use, remains as a central, underlying factor and the presumption that the pursuit of co-operation results in its disappearance is mistaken.

Working with establishments

In Chapter Three the value of preparing establishments for inspections was emphasised, involving the provision of information for all people who have an immediate interest in the inspection: users; relatives; staff and managers/owners.

There may be occasions on which it is useful to widen those who are informed of the inspection by including others such as health professionals in regular contact with the establishment (perhaps GPs, community nurses and health visitors), local police, hospitals, voluntary organisations or neighbours. If preparation is to be of value it has to be carried out sufficiently in advance for questions and anxieties to be checked out before the start of the inspection.

There are potential advantages arising from an inspection for a number of groups of people. Indeed, this highlights a significant aspect of inspection: it has different meanings in terms of opportunities and threats for different individuals and groups. For staff, the fact of having interested outsiders looking at and commenting on practice provides a hitherto rare opportunity for scrutiny of one's work. On occasions when I have been part of a group that is subject to inspection I have found that, whatever the anxiety, it is useful to talk about your work with other people. Indeed, when working as a teacher/housemaster in a residential school, an education inspector provided a rare interest in what I was doing and offered valuable advice about teaching techniques. For staff caught up in the minutiae of every day life, the inspectorate assessment can be beneficial for it provides an overview which puts some of the day to day concerns into context. Thus, a manager aware of all the shortfalls in her/his establishment which there are struggles to rectify, may find the overview helpful because it may highlight the solid achievements which it is easy to forget.

A later theme in this chapter is opening up inspections. This raises the core question of the extent to which inspectorate staff can be open with staff in the places which they inspect. Burton (1993, pp.148-9)) makes the case for inspectorates being explicit about their concerns. The aim is 'to ensure that this home is providing proper care' not to catch people out. Therefore, he argues, inspectors should tell managers of their concerns, for example that they are not convinced that staffing levels are always kept to the stated levels and that they will be calling unannounced to check during the next few weeks. I have heard a colleague inspector set out terms to a manager in precisely that way: 'You have agreed that you will not be trying to manage so many tasks in the evening and I shall call back to see how that is working'. Burton's core point is that in residential establishments there are powerful factors which create distrust: inspectorates should not adopt styles which reinforce the ideas of spying and catching out. Indeed, the point could be developed: inspectors should try to model good practice.

That is not to argue that on all occasions inspectors should make their concerns explicit. The general rule is that inspectorate staff should be open about the standards against which establishments (and people!) are judged, the inspection procedures, the rights of all parties, the ways to deal with concerns and complaints of those who are inspected and the nature of any anxieties that inspectors have and the ways in which those will be examined. However, there are exceptions: on occasions inspectors may be working with police to investigate a serious allegation of assault; it may be necessary not to let anyone know about the allegation until certain records have been seen and secured by police or inspectors. Even in extreme circumstances the general principle stands that inspectors will detail their concerns unless they have overriding reasons for not doing so; the 'overriding reasons' must not be used to avoid saying difficult things.

There is much talk of including outsiders on inspections. Comparatively little thought is given to whether staff from homes, schools and day care may be included in inspections. The local authority staff in Cumbria who were seconded into the inspectorate team for specific investigations or for specific periods of time (six months to two years) contributed a great deal to the understanding of regulation but also learnt about the characteristics of quality and how they are demonstrated. They took with them on leaving the inspectorate new understandings that were of use to their practice. A further gain is that there is increased understanding of the way in which the inspectorate works. The same would be true of seconding in staff from the independent sector.

Establishing authority

Another attribute is establishing authority. As much writing on authority makes clear, the word authority conveys both the formal authority that is ascribed to people in role and the way that authority is added to by what is built up between individuals. It is this latter aspect that systems can play a part in enhancing. The manner in which consultation is carried out, information is shared, and decisions are made and notified are important components in the establishment of authority. The procedures for these activities, in other words the systems which are in part the focus of this chapter, will contribute to the establishment of authority. The point being made is that while the skill, knowledge and style of inspectorates are important, so too is their efficiency in doing what they state. Thus for example, efficiency will be demonstrated at meetings with individuals and associations (such as the Pre School Playgroups' Association, or owners' and managers' associations), by whether or not the inspection unit has taken action in relation to points made at a previous meeting.

Working with colleague inspectors

Within the context of *working with others* is an aspect specific to life within the inspectorate, that of *working with colleague inspectors*. Inspectors are members of teams in a variety of ways:

1. as a member of a total unit;
2. as a member of a section, registering and inspecting similar facilities;
3. as a member of a team of two or more inspectors carrying out an inspection.

In relation to the first of these, the membership of the total group, individual staff should be working to fulfil the values and mission of the inspection unit. This requires an involvement in setting the strategy of the unit and in determining its objectives and procedures. Staff meetings and training are two mechanisms for accomplishing this. As with all other procedures about which I am writing the fact of holding the meetings does not achieve the objectives; what is critical is the conduct of the meetings.

As members of sections, staff are likely to take messages, deal with matters in colleagues' absence and on occasions carry out inspections in a facility usually inspected by someone else. It is vital that there is confidence between individuals and that differences of approach and opinion are handled carefully. Many of us will be familiar, either from the way we have behaved or have seen others, of the significance of the style of a newcomer on the scene. 'She/he said that...' often implies clearly that someone else has made an error of judgement though the individual making the comment rests in the belief that since an overt criticism of a colleague has been avoided, all is well.

A central issue in the third area, that of teams of inspectors, is the manner in which people work with each other in public. This has particular resonance in a residential establishment where staff have to manage the same type of issues far more frequently. They will be well tuned in to the vibrations arising from the way inspectors are working with each other, especially when together at more formal occasions such as introductory or feedback meetings. Preparation and rehearsal is necessary but does not dispense with the tension. I think the strength of the team is likely to be shown in the ways in which individuals deal with the very issues that were unexpected.

There are several scenarios of what might happen at such meetings: a manager says, 'I have been delighted with the way you have fitted in with the life of the place in general but I was very angry when I heard that X had...'; a staff member who comments that two inspectors have given conflicting interpretations of the inspectorate's own standards; a young person complaining that an inspector had been asking questions that were too intimate; or an inspector who, in the middle of a meeting, directs the feedback into an area that had been agreed amongst the team would not be raised because there other more pressing matters. The two most common reactions are either to leave the individual to fend for her or himself or to support the individual on the basis that the team stands or falls as a whole.

There are important underlying themes: loyalty to colleagues; trust in colleagues; the extent to which differences are allowed, openly or in secret, amongst individual inspectors, especially when the issue is fundamental; openness and honesty; the responsibilities given to individual inspectors, for example to lead an inspection or a part of it; understandings about working style. Working together in public requires understandings of how matters will be raised between colleagues during the meeting. These are some of the skills required in co-working in groups. For example it is possible to introduce new ideas or shift the direction of the discussion by talking directly to the colleague: 'I wondered whether you wanted to move on to...'; or 'There is a topic that I wanted to bring in, if you think this is the appropriate time...'. People who work well with each other sometimes say things more directly: 'I am not sure that we (or you!) explained that clearly...'; 'I am a bit confused by this; I had thought that... ; do you have a different interpretation?' Inspectors when working together on an inspection have to find ways of thinking collectively on their feet: getting ideas, having concerns and working out in public how to raise them.

Opening up inspection

The notion of opening up is hard to challenge: it presumes that things have been closed and hidden; therefore we have to assume that they should be made open, nurtured as we are in openness being lauded as a virtue, in word if not in practice. The core questions are: 'What is closed?' 'What is being opened up?' and 'For whose benefit?'.

The crux is the ambivalence towards regulation. Inspectorates have been created: but can they be trusted? That is not to argue that the work of inspection units should not be open to surveillance; it is only to point the fact that no amount of opening up procedures can solve the dilemma that regulators may regulate in ways that others dislike. What should be required of social care regulation is that:

- inspectorates are explicit about what is required of providers and the procedures that are used;
- there are means for interested parties to contribute to the debate about those standards and procedures;
- those who are most directly affected by and interested in inspection activities, know, first, how they may tell inspectors what they think about the quality of provision at particular places; *and*
- secondly, how they get information on the inspectors' judgements about that quality;
- outsiders have sufficient information to make judgements about the quality of the work of inspectorates.

The Department of Health (1994b, 1994c) has emphasised four aspects: involving the wider public in inspection; advisory panels; open reporting and follow up of inspection reports. Each of these is useful but each will create its own set of technical problems. None of them dispenses with the issue of trust. Thus, involving lay people in inspection has the potential to improve the quality of inspection activity: there are other perspectives than that of the in-house team and, perhaps most importantly, lay people will be able to see the processes of regulation. Brooke Ross (1993a) sets out what 'the principal benefits of lay involvement appear to be':

1. fresh eyes – different perspectives on individual homes and the application of standards to individual homes;
2. monitoring the even-handedness of inspection units and of individual inspectors;
3. validating and assisting judgements, and possible decisions about, individual homes' quality of life for residents and future residents;
4. assisting in setting standards and inspection procedures which affect providers and receivers of care (p.37).

She stresses (p.40) that 'lay inspectors should not be viewed as cheaper alternatives'. In her study, inspectors said that lay inspectors created more work for inspection units and inspectors, providers and lay inspectors all thought training essential. An intriguing question follows: what sort of training equips lay people to undertake the task without negating the very qualities of difference for which they were wanted in the first place.

Yet, there have to be checks on the lay people: they too may be drawn into the activity for personal gratification, for power or at worst to abuse vulnerable service users. They may write reports which are biased, offensive, (for example in terms of the Race Relations Act) or libellous. Is the local authority to contravene the standards laid down for its own activities and publish these? Once it is accepted that the 'common sense' of lay people does not allow them total freedom, a system has to be introduced for their selection, the monitoring of their work and, if needs be, their dismissal.

Some aspects are parallel to those existing with paid staff. Opportunities should be advertised; there should be criteria and procedures for selection; there have to be procedures for dealing with complaints about their work. Decisions have to be made about payment and expenses for lay assessors, recognising that not making any payment may limit the people who become lay assessors to set groups of people.

Writing such as this may seem defensive and designed to exclude outsiders. It is not intended to do that. I consider that including lay people in inspections is a valuable additional resource at inspection. However, it will only work properly if it is recognised that there will be additional costs in terms of administration and organisation. Further, once the decision has been made to regulate, nothing can remove the tension that is inherent in regulation – that regulators make judgements which some people will find unacceptable.

Publicity

Sometimes it is presumed that inspectorates will stop abuse, assuring a minimum standard of care. Frequently that will be the case: the existence of registration and inspection, with specified standards and requirements, will inhibit some people from opening day and residential facilities, will require improvements from some existing managers and will uncover and stop some bad practice. However, it is mistaken to think that inspectorates will prevent all abuse. Rather, inspection units should be expected to uncover abuse promptly and to take prompt action. One of the main mechanisms for uncovering abuse is through information from service users, their relatives and other visitors. It is vital for inspectorates that their existence is widely known so that anyone with anxieties will inform them of their concerns. Publicity is essential.

Such publicity may take many forms. It could cover: the public availability of inspection reports as an aid to choice for prospective users or knowledge of performance for current users; the location of inspectorate and other social services department offices where anxieties and complaints may be lodged; the existence of inspection advisory panels; committee reports, including the annual inspection report;

It is easy to write that certain information will be made publicly available; whether or not anybody uses the material will depend on the location of the information, how it is advertised, the language in which it is written and the ease with which it can be studied. Some inspectorates make their material available in public libraries and are considering whether lists of registered facilities, inspection reports, together with advice about how to choose a facility, could be made available through existing computer terminals. Even this brings out further tensions between a wish to have easy access to information and a wish to protect vulnerable users. Some people might want to use lists of day care facilities for young children to get improper access to children. The balance may be found by restricting certain details until individual enquirers provide identification. The significant point is that publicity, as openness, is not straightforward and has to be planned and managed.

MANAGEMENT OF INSPECTION

Systems need to be in place to support the following activities:

- collecting evidence;
- reviewing the evidence and the options;
- planning (identifying the gaps in knowledge about an establishment; pursuing 'lines of enquiry' as the police would say; managing the process of enquiry);
- recording; collecting further evidence;
- taking action (determining what to say and to whom);
- sharing information and opening up inspections;
- publicity about the activities of the inspectorate and about individual reports.

Each stage in the registration and inspection process throws up its own set of issues for which systems have to be developed. The extent to which the inspectorate achieves its objectives is likely to be found in the mechanisms (the procedures or systems) which it devises to cope with specific matters. At the collecting of evidence stage, inspectors have to be sure that the material will stand up to scrutiny and indeed to challenge. The nature and quality of the evidence, and the way in which it is recorded are all significant. For example, the type of record matters. Tape recordings, photocopies, written statements, file notes all have value but all have limitations. The procedures used by the police in using tape recording or in taking witness statements exist so that the information will stand up to scrutiny in court. Inspectorates must have systems for collecting information which will stand up to such scrutiny if that is needed. Indeed, the ability of the inspectorate staff to link their judgement with evidence will depend on the records that are kept.

There is a tendency to think of collecting evidence as a stage in preparing for a negative report. In fact it is neutral. The key question is: 'What is the available evidence which will inform the inspectorate as to the quality of provision at this establishment?' It is as important that an inspection unit has backing for a view that a place is 'satisfactory' or 'good' as it is that there is backing for conclusions that somewhere is 'unsatisfactory'. In the case of a report stating a facility is satisfactory, the inspectorate lays itself on the line in a similar way (though with different consequences) as it does with an 'unsatisfactory' verdict. Providing evidence to back a conclusion of adequacy may be essential in a situation where allegations have been made against an establishment, in particular because it may be suggested that the inspectorate had no reason to reach the judgement which it did.

One of the nightmare scenarios for inspectors is the later uncovering of abuse or poor practice in a place which they have inspected and judged satisfactory. The test for the inspectorate is whether or not it carried out its task thoroughly and whether it examined the evidence available and searched for contrary evidence. Having done that, it has to be accepted that inspections are not infallible: some people may know things that they choose not to talk about; inspections are only a snapshot. The inspection unit must have a system that:

1. ensures that its primary task of examining and making judgements is supported and carried out; and
2. records what has taken place – the procedures that were used in carrying out the inspection, the information that became available, and the way in which staff reviewed the material to reach their conclusions.

The difficulty with the argument I am putting forward is that it may seem like a defence for poor practice or like an assertion that the outcome does not matter provided the system has been properly administered. We are all too familiar with the protectiveness of professionals; I have already noted the belief of some staff in social services departments that what matters in child protection work is the efficiency in recording and following procedures, not the quality of the judgement. My point is that the critical test is whether the task was properly carried out, not whether records were kept properly.

CONCLUSION

It is in the establishment and working out of procedures for such activities that it can seem to individual staff or outsiders that what happens is driven by increasingly precise instructions over every aspect of work. It is here that we return to what may seem a paradox. Systems must be established to ensure that the grand ideas are realised, and that the expressed values are integral to the work; but these same systems must not drive the activities. At the heart of successful management in inspection as elsewhere is the way in which managers create an environment in which staff may work to their potential: it is essential that staff are able to challenge and question, be creative, be open. In effect, if the inspectorate cannot create a style of working amongst its own staff that builds confidence and trust, then it has no hope of creating such a style in its work with those it inspects.

People would construct varying lists of the components of management that would produce the best practice. Probably the catalogue would include factors like creating a climate in which people learn, trying not to ascribe fault, having the right mix of overview and detail, the best balance of team in terms of gender, race, specialism, age, culture that will develop into an appropriate blend of consistency and difference.

The management needs to work at five levels:

1. individuals;
2. culture, myths, values;
3. formal structures;
4. environment;
5. external pressures (managing the boundary).

Some systems are better than others to achieve desired objectives. It is in the detail that inspectors demonstrate their capacity or their incompetence and live out their values.

Eight

Is inspection worth the effort? The evaluation of inspection

Jean Bradshaw

SOCIAL SERVICES departments had had responsibility under the Registered Homes Act (1984) for the registration and inspection of residential care homes for adults. However, inspection units with their increased range of responsibilities were not required to be established until April 1991, so they are comparatively recent. By December 1992, only twenty months after the inspection units had been in existence, the Department of Health produced a document *Inspecting Social Services*, which brought into question the effectiveness of inspection units. In August 1993 the Department of Health (1993c) sought views on deregulation of homes for adults and this was followed in April (1994d) by proposals for a reduced level of inspection for boarding schools. It would seem that the government has little confidence in the effectiveness of inspection units. This contrasts with a statement made by Smith that the units have been one of the few success stories of community care implementation (Rickford, 1992, p.16).

Before looking in more depth at the factors that have led to the differing judgements of inspection units, it would be useful to explore how the effectiveness of inspection is to be judged or measured.

WHAT IS EFFECTIVENESS?

The Audit Commission (1984) states 'Effectiveness may be defined as how well a programme or activity is achieving its established goals or other intended effects' (Section 40). This presupposes that the goals and intended effects are clearly defined and understood and can be easily assessed. In addition, it takes no account of unintended effects and may not address the overall impact of the programme on the recipients' quality of life or even the quality of care offered in the programme.

A broader definition of effectiveness is given by Beattie (1989):

> ...effectiveness ... is concerned with crucial issues of the longer-term external outcomes of the programme: what its social impact is, what changes it effects in the health of its clients, what positive achievements in the wider environment can be explicitly credited to the work undertaken, etc (p.7).

Using this concept of effectiveness, assessment becomes much more complex as it necessitates the identification of all the outcomes of the programme, intended and unintended, direct and indirect, as well as the establishment of the link between cause and effect. Goldberg and Connelly (1982, p.12) describe the problems of measuring the success or failure of outcome in social care settings and Challis and colleagues (1984, p.125) emphasise the complexity of evaluation when issues like well-being and quality of life are being considered.

This makes the task of assessing effectiveness hard enough. A further dimension is introduced by a scientific approach based on positivism which would claim that such assessment should be possible because it is an objective exercise, in search of the truth, which is verifiable fact. One problem with this approach is that the methodology is often inadequate to determine the truth (Guba and Lincoln, 1989; Bryman 1988). If the positivist paradigm is replaced by the constructivist paradigm then there is no absolute truth, and definitions of truth, facts, causes and effect exist only as defined by the people concerned (Guba and Lincoln, 1989, pp.44 & 83). This leads to the obvious conclusion that there is no objectivity in evaluation, since every part of the process involves value judgements (Feek, 1988, p.6; Thomas, 1984, p.14; Barnes, 1993, p.48). As Cheetham and colleagues state (1992, p.145), the study of effectiveness of social work is inextricably linked with moral, social and political questions. Roger Clough has suggested in Chapter Five that the requirement for the inspector may be 'disciplined subjectivity' rather than 'objectivity'.

All of this may seem to be straying from the subject, but it has been explored here to demonstrate the problems of defining effectiveness in relation to any aspect of social care. It has also identified some of the issues and dilemmas that will be explored in this chapter.

WHAT IS THE PURPOSE OF INSPECTION?

Defining the purpose of inspection is not simple. When exploring this within Cumbria's inspection unit, there was a debate amongst the staff about whether the purpose was to implement the legislation (as laid down in the Registered Homes Act 1984 and the Children Act 1989), to improve the quality of services, or to improve the quality of life of service users. The conclusion of this debate was embodied in the mission statement of the Inspection Unit which is 'to safeguard and promote the well-being of people who use social care services'. It was decided that implementing the legislation was a means of achieving the purpose; improving the quality of the service was one aspect of the work but the primary focus must be the impact on the service users. This debate moved beyond the simpler Audit Commission definition of effectiveness towards that given by Beattie, raising a multitude of questions about how effectiveness of a service and of an inspectorate could be assessed. Before even attempting to address this issue, I shall consider other statements which have been made about the purpose of inspection.

The Department of Health's (1990b) training pack *Making Sense of Inspection* which was produced prior to the establishment of 'arms length' inspection units, states that inspection consists of three elements: ensuring standards are being met; assessing the likely quality of life of residents; and judging the effectiveness of the home's management systems. In the following year, when the new inspection units were established, the Department of Health Policy Guidance (1991) was published. This gives three initial tasks for inspection units: to evaluate the quality of care provided and the quality of life experienced in private, voluntary and local authority residential establishments; to ensure a consistent approach between sectors; and to respond to the demands for quality control created by the growth in contracted-out service provision. These two documents give us a number of measures of effectiveness for inspection but both include the quality of life of service users.

Hudson (1993) stresses the same aspect:

> ...on ethical and effectiveness grounds, the experiences and perceptions of those who receive a service provide a better criterion for judging that service than those of service providers (p.5).

In the case of inspection, it is not easy to define who are the ones receiving the service but this does not negate the point being made.

In developing a quality system for the inspection unit in Cumbria, various customers were asked what they required of the service. Owners, manager, staff, service users, carers, professionals from other agencies, colleagues within Social Services, County Councillors and the general public were all seen as customers or potential customers and sampled in this exercise. A vast amount of information came out of this exercise which was eventually grouped into five key areas. The first was the production of understandable, accurate and useful information that would be easily available and reflect the views of service users. The second expectation referred to the inspection process, where clear and consistent standards, decisions and reports were required. Thirdly, customers wanted the inspection unit to be courteous, accessible, accurate, and up to date in all areas of work. The fourth area emphasised the importance of the inspection unit valuing its customers and giving them opportunities to comment on and evaluate the work of the unit. The last requirement was for the inspection unit to work from a clearly defined value base and be at the forefront of professional knowledge.

What people require of a service may not be quite the same as what they would use to judge its effectiveness but there must be some strong links between the two.

Another way to gauge the expectations of customers of inspectorates is to consider the responses of proprietors and managers to the proposals for deregulation of residential care and the introduction of new regulatory procedures for domiciliary care. Drawing on local and national information, it would seem that some consider inspection is based on regulations that are cumbersome and restrictive to the development of business. This group would prefer there to be no inspections but, if these are necessary, then they should be designed to minimise the inconvenience for service providers and users. The Social Services Inspectorate in their assessment of inspection units have a similar standard (Department of Health, 1993a, p.41). Others aspire to very high standards and are requesting a grading system, because they are not satisfied with meeting the minimum standards set by inspection units. They hope that this system will identify good practice in a detailed and systematic way and will show which establishments achieve levels of competence above the minimum.

The other important group of people are service users and their carers. Hudson (1993) points out that:

> ...although the Department of Health is keen for providers to have a voice within the system, it is even more emphatic that users should be more centrally placed than in the past (pp.4-5).

In similar vein Kelly (1990) writes, 'It is enticing to contemplate inspection units as the Trojan horse for the empowerment of service users'. If those were the dreams, we may now be in a position to assess the extent to which users have influenced the work of inspectorates. The Advisory Committees were one method designed to achieve this but in some areas users are playing a limited role in these committees. A committee tends to be a formal setting, with papers and procedures that are alien to many service users. Transport and access problems may also be a deterrent as may a lack of training or explanation of what the proceedings are about. The Department of Health's (1994b and 1994) Circular and Practice Guidance attempt to address some of these issues by increasing the numbers of lay people, in particular of users and carers on committees which are now to be called panels. In addition, the need to demystify and simplify the proceedings are highlighted. In Cumbria various strategies have been adopted: training sessions for committee members, separate meetings for young people, pre-meetings for members of the committees. Another way forward is that of involving users in the inspection process and this has been achieved in some areas and may be the most valuable group to include as 'lay assessors'.

Currently, users' views about the role of inspection are limited and are built up from individual comments such as the ones quoted in a recent annual report of an inspection unit, the last of which has already been quoted in Chapter 6:

> Thank you for the sensitive way you carried out the inspection.

> Inspectors should concentrate on our rights and not on our menus.

Inspectors should visit more often.

Thank you for getting the new shower curtains.

We feel there is no need for a daily register in everyday life ... we are not children and we would like you to take this into consideration please.

(Cumbria County Council, 1994, passim).

Both Kelly and Hudson emphasise the need to involve service users in setting and monitoring standards and they identify the central purpose of inspection as making judgements about the quality of care and the quality of life as experienced by the service users. Kelly (1990) continues:

...it is naive to believe that such characteristics of residential services can be assured by inspection ... monitoring and evaluation by inspection is simply a later stage of checking and judging outcomes (p.14).

HOW IS THE EFFECTIVENESS OF INSPECTION ASSESSED?

A truly effective inspection unit would safeguard and promote the well-being of service users – but how would this be assessed? If this well-being is reflected in the quality of care and the quality of life of service users, can this be assessed, and if it can, how has inspection contributed to these quality indicators? If, even this level of assessment is not possible, then maybe outcome cannot be assessed, but output could be measured, and efficient and effective systems and processes of inspection may give a reasonable indication of the overall effectiveness of inspection.

Following pilot inspections of inspection units in 1992-1993, the Social Services Inspectorate set a timetable to inspect all other units. Nine standards were used for this purpose (Department of Health, 1993a). These relate to policy, management, workload and resources, service standards, conduct of inspections, efficiency and effectiveness, inspection reports, inspection follow-up, and collaboration. Most of these refer to the systems and processes of inspection and not the outcome. Even when focusing on the Social Services Inspectorate standard on efficiency and effectiveness, the indicators refer to the efficiency and effectiveness of the process and the use of resources not the effectiveness of the outcome of inspection. Inspection units are being assessed against clear criteria, which do address such issues as the monitoring of standards, the effectiveness of the homes' management system and the consistency of approach across sectors but do not give any real evidence of the effectiveness of inspection in terms of the way inspection contributes to the quality of care or the quality of life of residents. Just as inspection units assume good systems in inspected establishments lead to good care and good quality of life, the Social Services Inspectorate use the assessments of the systems used by inspection units as the method of assessing their effectiveness. This is a theory explored in an article by Gibbs and Sinclair (1992b) who demonstrate the links between good systems and the outcomes of care in residential homes.

The findings of the Social Services Inspectorate Reports (Department of Health, 1993a, 1994a) on inspections of inspection units are worthy of some consideration. The reports indicate that the ten social services departments' inspection units visited in 1992-93 and the twenty seven visited in 1993-94 were making good progress against the standards set by the Social Services Inspectorate, including two units in the later sample that met all the standards. Some positive and negative issues are identified for comment here.

All SSDs had made good progress towards establishing management arrangements which accorded with the main objectives of government policy. All had established inspection units and advisory committees as required. All had set up units which were structurally separate from the service provider arm of the SSDs. Seven had set up their units in separate office locations. The heads of the inspection unit were of appropriate status within the local authority (Department of Health, 1993a p.2).

All of this fits the government's guidelines, but does it ensure effective inspection?

One indicator that might indicate effectiveness is whether or not targets set by the social services departments for the frequency of inspection matched or exceeded statutory requirements: only two inspectorates achieved the frequency targets required by legislation in 1992/93, although all units expected to be able to reach these targets by 1993-94. However, the Social Services Inspectorate was concerned about the impact of financial constraint on social services departments and hence on inspection units. In the 1993-94 inspection, only one third of inspection units, nine out of twenty seven, achieved all statutory and advisory frequency targets for inspection of residential homes; in all but a handful of units progress was very slow towards the expectation that day care for children under eight would be inspected at least once per year (Department of Health, 1994a, p.12).

All inspection units visited had produced or were developing service standards. Service providers had been consulted in the production of these standards but consultation with users was rare. It seems that an opportunity to ensure inspection was focused on the quality issues identified by users had been missed. The standards were applied equally to local authority and independent sector providers but only two social services departments had made a public commitment to ensure that inspection findings were implemented in both sectors. This disparity in which one sector may ignore the findings of an inspection has a crucial impact on the effectiveness of inspection. The Social Services Inspectorate also comment that the quality of the inspection reports varied and not all were available for publication. Well written and presented reports that are available to members of the general public must improve the impact of an inspection and its effectiveness. The Department of Health (1994c) has specified measures related to consultation and publication of reports.

The conclusion of the Social Services Inspectorate was

that social services departments had made good progress towards achieving the policy objectives of the government but there was no conclusion drawn about the effectiveness of the units.

WHAT OTHER MEASURES OF EFFECTIVENESS CAN BE FOUND?

What evidence is there that inspection has achieved anything? There is hard evidence available in the form of home closures, prosecutions of owners and changes enforced by Registered Homes' Tribunal decisions. In addition there are more and more complaints for inspection units to investigate; some have been unfounded but many have led to modifications in practice. The most serious complaints may lead to homes closing. It could be argued that complaints should not be necessary if inspection is really effective. The counter argument is that complaints are coming to inspection units because the credibility and effectiveness of the unit is recognised.

The effectiveness of inspection could also be assessed by reading successive inspection reports, or visiting establishments or facilities after a time lapse and seeing what changes have taken place. There is no doubt that alterations have been made. A study of inspection reports or visits to homes would show that minimum standards have been achieved in homes that were below standard: facilities such as the number of single occupancy or en suite rooms have improved; similarly it would also be possible to show other improvements such as the introduction of care planning or staff training.

The first question that would have to be asked before these changes could be seen as examples of the effectiveness of inspection, relates to whether these changes can be attributed to inspection process. It may be claimed that these changes are as a result of market forces, or the introduction of the NHS and Community Care Act or Children Act, or the general improvement in standards brought about by reports such as Wagner (1988) or Howe (1992). There might be some examples where the link between inspection report and improvement stands out: for example a recommendation in one report might have been carried out by the next.

The other question that would have to be addressed is whether these changes are safeguarding and promoting the well-being of service users of even improving their quality of life. There certainly would be evidence that some of the changes improve the quality of care for residents but whether en suite facilities improve quality of life may vary from individual to individual. The facilities in some homes may have improved remarkably, but this may have a created a plush hotel type atmosphere which some residents find makes them feel uncomfortable and they do not feel it is at all homely. What are assessed as improvements in care practices by professionals may not be what individual residents want. In assessing the effectiveness of inspection great care has to be taken about claiming progress has been made if it does not address the needs and preferences of the individual.

There is an opportunity for a research project to assess what changes can be attributed to inspection and how these changes safeguard and promote the well-being of service users.

EFFECTIVE INSPECTIONS

If it is correct that some of the changes are attributable to inspection and that they do safeguard and promote the well-being of service users, a question follows as to the best means for inspectorates to achieve such influence. Is it via encouragement or enforcement, or is it a case of the carrot and the stick? Is the best method different in the independent sector from that in the local authority sector?

Hudson (1993) states: 'There is some tension between the dual role of IUs (inspection units) to inspect on the one hand, and offer advice and support on the other' (p.3). On the other hand, the official Policy Guidance notes: 'Over-emphasis on one or other approach is unlikely to serve the best interests of units or service providers' (Department of Health, 1991).

This is endorsed by Beck (1991): 'But make no mistake, after praising the positive aspects of a residential establishment the inspector's report should include a discussion of the shortcomings of the home and identify areas for change' (p.22).

She goes on to say that inspectors should act as a catalyst for change and this is stressed in the Department of Health Policy Guidance when it states that one of the main objects of the inspection is to inform service development. How to achieve this is a matter of judgement for inspectors and requires a knowledge of individual proprietors and staff groups to identify the most productive strategy but the Practice Guidance is quite clear that where conflict arises between the inspectorial and supportive roles, the inspector role must come first (Department of Health, 1991). Gibbs and Sinclair (1992b, pp.464-65) identify the difficulties in taking action over poor practice because evidence will need to stand up before a tribunal; if the evidence is sound and the case is upheld, there is the problem of what will happen to the service users if the registration of the home is cancelled. For these reasons and because of the problems of consistency in inspection Gibbs and Sinclair (1992b, p.465) state that it is more important to concentrate on taking steps to improve a home than taking action when matters have gone wrong.

Considerable emphasis has been given to consideration of the effectiveness of inspection being demonstrated by changes in practice. There is a danger in this approach of measuring inspection in part by the action that others take, rather than the action that is taken by the inspectorate. As with the police, an inspectorate might prepare a good case for a proposal to refuse registration, only to have a Tribunal refuse to endorse the proposal. I would argue that another measure of an effective inspectorate is a willingness to take action when practice is poor and has not been improved. Of course, it is difficult to monitor in terms of effectiveness but there is a legitimate task for inspectorates, having properly reviewed whether alternative action is feasible, to take formal action. When this is the case, the effective inspectorate will prepare its evidence and its case well. The point being stressed is that following Gibbs and Sinclair's line of concentrating on taking steps to improve an establishment must not lead inspectorates to thinking that implementing formal proceedings is either not feasible or, necessarily, a mark of the failure of the inspectorate.

There seems to be support for both the enabling and the enforcing roles of inspection but there is a difference of opinion about where the emphasis should be placed and a question mark over whether the two roles can be combined. It has been argued in Chapter Five that primacy of task has to be given to the regulatory functions of assessing, making judgements based on evidence and determining the action to be taken. Development and support may be a part of that process or an addition. The prime role is that of inspector, not developer.

The skill and judgement of the individual inspector come into play when determining how to act on evidence from inspections. The exercise of this skill should be in the context of procedures for management review of the work of inspectors.

The second issue raised at the beginning of this section was whether effectiveness of the inspectorate would be achieved differently in the local authority sector and the independent sectors. Despite all the talk of 'even-handedness', there is the fundamental difference that residential homes in the local authority are not required to register and therefore their registration cannot be cancelled. Local authority homes could be closed by the authority but this usually happens for financial reasons or because of changing needs or a major scandal and not because of steps taken by inspection units. As stated earlier the Social Services Inspectorate's inspection of ten local authorities identified only two which had taken steps to ensure that the findings from inspections would be implemented in the same way in the local authority and independent sectors (Department of Health 1993a, p.4); by the time of the second report, half the units inspected had met this standard

(Department of Health, 1994a, p.23). In addition the report stated that few social services departments had developed procedures for communication between inspection units and the department's own service managers for discussing the issues arising from inspection. One means of establishing procedures is by producing guidance for staff of both inspectorate and residential homes on what happens before during and after inspections (an example of this was developed by Cumbria Social Services, 1993).

Much of the guidance laid down for inspection units was to ensure that inspection units were 'arms length' from the provider function of the social services department. Many independent sector providers do not believe that there is an 'arms length' approach. The Social Services Inspectorate did state that 'unit inspectors had applied standards with equal force in relation to both local authority and independent sector services' (Department of Health, 1993a, p.5), but as Hudson (1993) comments:

> Many local authority homes are simply not up to the physical standard required for registration in the non-statutory sector, and at a time of general spending constraint and poll tax capping, IUs (inspection units) may be put under enormous pressure to moderate their findings (p.4).

The government consultative document *Inspecting Social Services* was motivated by a lack of confidence in the independence of inspection units and a desire to move them outside social services departments. Even though in the response to the consultation it was decided not to take this step, inspection units were put on 'trial' for two years with the understanding that a move may still be made at the end of this period. In addition, the response proposed the introduction of lay assessors into inspection, with the emphasis that lay assessors should be involved in all inspections of local authority homes. This seems a clear indication that the government does not believe in the even-handedness of inspection units. Despite this, the simplest method of ensuring equivalence would be to make the legislation apply to all sectors in the same way. This has been done for day nurseries, where local authority day nurseries have to register in the same way as independent sector ones.

CONCLUSION

There is evidence of the improvement of standards in day and residential establishments since the introduction of inspection but no proof that this can be attributed directly to the process of inspection. The very existence of inspectorates may play a part in changing the climate in which places operate so that they determine that it is in their interests to change the way they work. It is difficult to gauge the extent to which it is the existence of inspectorates or their active intervention which creates the alteration. Even if inspection may take credit for contributing to this improvement in standards, the effectiveness of inspection may not be demonstrated. That depends on how effectiveness is judged. Improving standards may not be the only way to assess effectiveness; it may be that improving the quality of life for service users is more important. Measuring this and assessing the contribution of inspection to it, is complex and opens up opportunities for further research.

This chapter may have raised more questions than it has answered but it has attempted to demonstrate the contribution that good inspection can make to the well-being of service users.

Nine

Analysis for action: the heart of inspection

Roger Clough

THE ACTIVITY OF REGULATION

'Tourists don't know where they've been', I thought.
'Travellers don't know where they're going'.

THUS THEROUX (1992, p.4) muses on his own travels. At the end of this book I reflect on the nature of inspection and the part I have played in it. What sort of journey is it that inspectors undertake? Is inspection at heart a solitary activity, with others as companions for short spells? How intrusive is inspection into the lives of the people who live there when the tourist/traveller/inspector has departed? Should inspection be seen as a type of colonial activity in which, overtly or more subtly, the views of the colonists are imposed? I am aware that analogies may be fun to play with for the individual toying with ideas but boring for others, as comparisons are pushed to extremes. Nevertheless, I think that there is use in drawing on Theroux's words to consider the nature of regulatory activity, the way it intrudes into the lives of others and the part it plays in wider systems.

Regulation demands conformity to rules. Once it is accepted that there is to be regulation, questions have to be asked about the construction of the components of regulation: what aspects of practice are to be subject to regulation? what are the rules (or standards) to be? what are the processes by which regulation will be carried out?

However, there is an earlier issue: whose interests are served by regulation? People who go on holiday to other places may reflect on the reasons: is it that they are unable to relax at home or that 'going away for a holiday' has become an expected part of everyday life. Yet, as we all know with some discomfort, the effects of our visiting other places destroys the naturalness and the otherness which we travelled to see. Inspectors, as others interested in regulation, have to ask themselves about the function and consequences, intended or not, of their activities. If regulation is a necessary adjunct of capitalism, existing to sell more products because people are convinced of their safety or quality, does that make a difference to the appropriateness of the regulation of day and residential care being carried out under the auspices of social services departments? Are inspectors playing a part in promoting provision about the very existence of which they have doubts, be they about residential homes for children or adults, boarding schools or early morning to evening day care for young children? What if regulation does impose, colonial style, inappropriate requirements on people who live and work in establishments?

I am not attempting to answer the questions, though I want to continue to study them. At a policy level it is essential that consideration is given to the role of social services departments not only as purchasers and providers but also as regulators. At an inspection unit or individual level, staff have to determine whether this activity is compatible with their own wider social care values. These are questions of the same order as those that face staff about the controlling nature of child care work or residential homes, together with the functions that they as workers are fulfilling for society. My point is that this sort of searching must not be shelved for inspection on the mistaken basis that this is a technical activity.

My framework for examining the issue is that the function of social care is to respond to people's present pain as well as to plan for change which will reduce the potential for such pain in the future. So my question becomes whether, social services staff should be involved in the regulation of social care provision, given that some of that provision is damaging and that other could be improved. My own answer is that they should.

STUDYING THE PRACTICE OF OTHERS

The traveller/tourist analogy is helpful also in thinking about the different ways in which we look at the activities of others, try to understand the characteristics of their lives and suggest explanations for what we perceive. Indeed, the same features exist for researchers. What is common to the traveller (at least in Theroux's reflective style), researcher and inspector is that they are outsiders who think that being an outsider assists them in assessment and analysis of what they see. There are substantial differences in the motivation of these groups of people with, I suspect, the traveller far more using the experience of difference to think about self and home. The issue being considered here though is the validity of their perspective on the total composition of what life may be said to be like in that place. It is arguable also that insiders, bounded as they are by virtue of the fact of being an insider, sometimes rarely moving away from the place where they live, also have limits to their perception. Do older residents of residential homes put up with life styles that they do not like because they think that is how a residential home has to be, because they recognise that the most significant aspect of their lives is living with personal losses which they did not want or because they are unwilling to complain?

It is useful to remind ourselves that in the same way as inspectors' views and judgements are not absolutes, nor are those of the people who live and work there. Earlier I have described inspection as a series of snapshots: individual residents and staff also provide snapshots related to their feelings at a particular time; these snapshots are a part of the composite picture.

Some would say that the only way to understand another is to walk in his or her shoes. The task for the inspector is not to understand an individual but a facility, a residential home, school or day care service. Even if an inspector wishes, the task of 'walking in the shoes of a facility' is an impossibility. What we are faced with is the myriad perspectives on the service and the consequent task for inspectors to extend their own view by walking some way in the shoes of several others. Following this, the task is to paint a picture (or perhaps more accurately a series of pictures) which captures sufficient of the generality while acknowledging that some see things differently: in the main the place or the service appears like this though some see it like that. Unlike the traveller, the inspector, an outsider trying to hold the totality of what is perceived, must neither focus on a single aspect because of its interest and ignore others, nor impose an idiosyncratic perspective.

SPY OR STATISTICIAN?

Increasingly, people who are assessors of others' work publish both the criteria for assessment and the procedures for carrying out the inspection. Yet, as researchers rapidly find out, people reveal aspects of their work which have a significance for the researcher of which those being studied are unaware; there is an outsider's agenda with which the insider cannot be totally familiar. There is a limit to the extent to which the outsider can explain the subtlety of the way in which detail provides clues to culture and style. Even when every attempt is being made to explain details the insider has not the experience of walking in the assessor's shoes. Thus what may be clues to the person making the assessment may not appear significant to the person being observed. Indeed, a part of the importance to the assessor is that some aspects are taken for granted by the insider.

An obvious example is the way in which staff address users or the manner in which a visitor is shown around an establishment. One person forms conclusions, knowing that clues are being given unwittingly by others. When reports use this information to draw conclusions about quality of practice, often staff feel betrayed. This person to whom they showed themselves has used the information to draw what they consider to be inappropriate conclusions. Of course this suggests a degree of naivety which does not exist. The knowledge that you are being observed by another affects your behaviour even if the response to observation is a determined effort to be no different than usual. What cannot be specified for or prescribed are the conclusions one person will draw from the observation of another.

Inspectors are doing more than collecting data; they are interpreting the data. At one end of a continuum are situations where there is minimal interpretation, such as the measurement of rooms. Even in those circumstances, an inspector will have to decide how to record information where a room is not perfectly square. More typically, indicators are used which have to be interpreted in the light of the use to which the indicator was being put. Without interpretation, reports will miss the essentials; with interpretation, reports run the danger of distorting.

In their significant work on analysis of regimes in hospitals and residential homes, King, Raynes and Tizard (1971) used different schedules to test for institutionalised practice. A part of one schedule, designed to look at rigidity of routine, examined whether children got up and went to bed at the same time at weekends as they did during the week. Inevitably, a place where there were not changes at weekends would be judged to have a rigid routine: yet it is possible that some children might want to get up at the same time at weekends or that the weekday regime was flexible enough for weekends. The data need interpretation.

So, recognising that inspectors must interpret the information they collect, we have to consider the extent to which their activities will seem devious to those being inspected. It seems probable that the more congruity of expectation of regulation there is between different parties, the less likelihood there is that inspectors will be seen either as spies, in that covertly they collected their findings, or as manipulators, in that they select (and risk distorting) their information.

The act of inspecting has as an imperative the searching out of the 'truth' or, reworded, the revelation of life as it really is. The investigator has considerable authority in a formal sense and a moral sense. Thus an inspector, if asked to leave the premises by a manager, may comment that she/he will do so but has the authority to be there by virtue of legislation and will record that she/he has been asked to leave. As powerful an argument in a different way, is that used by other investigators such as the police: 'I am only here to note what I see; if you have nothing to hide, what can be your concern at my looking around?' What is wrong with this approach is that it is trying to use the moral high ground to get people to give up their rights.

Another aspect of investigation is that as with other inspection activity, it has the potential to generate excitement. The inspector is at the centre of events, has a task the outcome from which has considerable significance for the people in the place being inspected, and may enjoy the hunt for the truth. Indeed, looking at what others are doing may become voyeuristic.

EXTENT OF INVASIVENESS

To find out what is going on inspectors must intrude into the life of the place: they cannot sit back and wait for information to be passed to them. Their task is to reach their own conclusions and in so doing to get behind the front. It is a task that requires a measure of disturbance. As has been indicated in different chapters of this book, one approach can be to allow users and staff some space to tell their story of the place in the way that they wish. A variety of mechanisms can also be used: questionnaires, interviews, studies of files and records, participant observation, other written material from individuals such as diaries. Any of these can be adapted, for example with questionnaires by varying the length or having different style of required response from ticking boxes to sentence completion. Whatever the method, the soliciting of information may be disturbing. Some people will be reminded of their dissatisfaction with their present life; others may find certain questions trigger disturbing trains of thought.

The inspector needs to know this, but cannot inspect without being invasive either to the general life and privacy within the place as a whole or to individuals. Nor is it possible, nor should, an inspector attempt to censor any question which might upset someone: there is no way of knowing what has the potential to create upset. What the inspector must do is to work out what information is essential and then to decide the best ways to collect the material.

The recognition that inspection must be intrusive does not justify riding rough shod over the life style of an establishment and the wishes of individuals. For example, inspectors have right of access to records but residents might not want their personal information to be seen. As was suggested in Chapter Three such matters may be resolved satisfactorily in discussion between inspectors, users and staff. The inspector has to work out what it is that access to a resident file might show: for example, the extent to which there is a personalised programme or life style for the individual; the ways in which staff write about users; the details of health care or financial arrangements; any complaints or anxieties. Having done this, there are options to consider: to get access to such information in other ways, to see parts of the file, or to note a decision not to examine this material.

MAKING JUDGEMENTS AND INTERVENTION

Judgements, as has been stated earlier, are not to be seen as neutral and technical; they are conditioned by values. The values should be made explicit because the acknowledgement that inspection is a value based task leads inevitably to a conclusion that the values of some people might be considered to be unacceptable. The same applies to lay assessors.

Values are also drawn on in determining what to do with the information that is produced. The task of inspection is at least as much to be able to act as to explain; inspectorates need a drive for action; they must be able and expect to intervene. Whatever the reason that may account for what is happening the inspector has to determine both whether practice is acceptable and what action is to be taken.

The rules and procedures may give guidance but do not decide on individual responses. In discussions of the refereeing in the 1994 football World Cup, commentators have made statements that people have become too rule bound, that they are failing to interpret the rules or that they have become fearful that if they do not act in accordance with the precise specification they will not be asked to referee at any more matches. The issue is that of rules, discretion, interpretation and action; a part of this is caught in the phrase about 'the letter rather than the spirit of the law'. Decisions about action in inspection should be made in the context of judgements and values by assessing the current state of the establishment, the degree of risk or problem, the overview or history of the place and the available options. Such decisions ought not to be the type of defensive reaction when action is taken 'to cover our backs'.

The complexity of the assessment and decision making stands out: what are the ultimate standards (if there are any) against which the detail is tested? On occasions inspectors will come across practices or daily life arrangements which, to them at least, are unusual: what determines if they are to be regarded as problematic or idiosyncratic and, perfectly proper, maybe even interesting?

If there is judged to be bad practice, is it a pocket in a place that is otherwise satisfactory or pervasive? How much of a risk does it seem to be to say that a place is good? Inspection gathers together information on specifics: in looking at the parts do you get a picture that is less than the whole?

There are situations where an inspector judges practice to be unsatisfactory but a resident says that it is all right. In such circumstances the inspector has to determine whether there is a requirement or responsibility to intervene. In most situations in 'ordinary' life outside inspection, adults decide whether or not they wish to take action against another; and the law allows action on behalf of another only if that person is judged to be incapable of protecting her or himself. Does the existence of registration in effect acknowledge the vulnerability of users and thus pass responsibility for deciding whether or not to intervene to the inspector? There is a wider aspect: the protection and quality of life for future users. In part the dilemma is whether or not taking action in the interests of others demeans their responsibilities.

THE TELLING OF STORIES

At the end of the performance, whether the writing of this book or an inspection, we can look back on the way the story was told. There is no inevitability in the telling. People choose points to start and to end, they draw on illustrations for their text, they determine what is to be included and what left out. The information for the story is collected in various ways but if the story is to have any life and be sensitive to the difference from the story that was told about somewhere else, like Theroux's traveller, the story teller must absorb what is happening and wander in a different direction than had been planned.

In the process, the inspector listens to others 'telling tales' or 'telling stories'. Wholesome inspection demands that the ways in which inspectors collect the information for their report are ones which promote the very qualities which the inspectorate thinks matter in establishments: they are concerned with the nature of relationships, the way inspectors talk to and about others, their willingness to listen, their ability to be aware of their own feelings but not to be consumed or driven by them. They should explain to people who want to talk to them about unpleasant events, (*telling tales* as bullies would describe it), that the responsibility for the event rests with the perpetrator.

IN THE END...

In the end, inspectors and others have to consider whether the job was done well. As inspectors, can we specify what we would like written on our epitaphs, or, closer to the present, the characteristics by which we would want to be judged? Inspectors may be viewed as the conscience of the organisation, with people waiting to see them fail to meet the standards they look for in others. That creates the temptation to hide mistakes and cover up. Inspectors have to live with their frailty more openly than most. Knowing that they will not always be right, either in analysis or action, there is an imperative to assess and to do something – to make judgements and to act. The inspector is not an accidental tourist nor an armchair traveller.

Bibliography

Ager, A. (1990) *Life Experiences Checklist*. NFER Nelson.

Allen, I., Hogg, D. and Peace, S. (1992) *Elderly People: Choice, Participation and Satisfaction*. London: Policy Studies Institute.

Audit Commission (1984) *Code of Local Government Audit Practice for England and Wales*. London: HMSO.

Barbier A. (1994) *Young People's Views of Cumbria Social Services*. Unpublished Report.

Barnes, M. (1993) 'Introducing new stakeholders - user and researcher interests in evaluation', *Policy and Politics*, 21(1), pp.47-58.

Beattie, A. (1989) 'From quantity to quality? The four E's of evaluation', *Community Health Action*, 12(Spring), pp.7-9.

Beck, J. (1991) 'Measure for measure', *Social Work Today*, 30 May, p.22.

Beedell, C. (1983) Unpublished lectures, Bristol

Brooke Ross, R. (undated) *Joint Working in Inspection by Health Authorities and Local Authorities*. London: Centre for Inner City Studies, University of London.

Brooke Ross, R. (1993a) *Lay Involvement in Inspection in England*. London: Centre for Inner City Studies, University of London.

Brooke Ross, R. (1993b) *Users, Advisory Committees and Inspection Units, Centre for Inner City Studies*. London: University of London.

Brown, A. and Clough, R. (1989) *Groups and Groupings: Life and Work in Day and Residential Centres*. London: Tavistock.

Bryman, A. (1988) *Quantity and Quality in Social Research*. London: Unwin Hyman.

Burton, J. (1993) *The Handbook of Residential Care*. London: Routledge.

Caring in Homes Initiative (1992) *Inside Quality Assurance.* London: Centre for Environmental and Social Studies in Ageing.

Centre for Policy on Ageing (1986) *Home Life: A Code of Practice for Residential Care.* London: Centre for Policy on Ageing.

Challis, D., Knapp, M. and Davies, B. (1984) 'Cost effectiveness evaluation of social work services' in Lishman, J. (ed.) *Evaluation.* Research Highlights Number Eight. Aberdeeen: Department of Social Work, University of Aberdeen.

Challis, L, (1990) *Organising Public Services.* Harlow: Longman.

Cheetham, J., Fuller, R., McIvor, G. and Petch, A. (1992) *Evaluating Social Work.* Milton Keynes: Open University Press.

Chisnall, P (1991) *The Essence of Market Research.* London: Prentice Hall.

Clough, R. (1981) *Old Age Homes.* London: Allen and Unwin.

Clough, R. (1982) *Residential Work.* Basingstoke: Macmillan.

Clough, R. (1987) *Living Away from Home: A Report on Research into Residential Child Care for the ESRC.* Bristol: University of Bristol.

Clough, R. (1990) *Practice, Politics and Power in Social Services Departments.* Aldershot: Gower.

Clough, R. (1992) *Methods of Consultation in Residential Care Homes. Report for Joint meeting of North and South Consultative Forums, 14. July.* Carlisle: Cumbria Social Services.

Cumbria County Council, (1993a) *Annual Report and Business Plan, Cumbria Social Services Inspectorate.* Carlisle: Cumbria Social Services.

Cumbria County Council (1993b) *Implications of Requiring Local Authority Residential Homes To Be Subjected to the Same Procedure Following Inspections as Independent Sector Homes. Social Services Inspection Panel, 1 December (Agenda Item 11).* Carlisle: Cumbria Social Services.

Cumbria County Council, (1994) *Annual Report and Business Plan, Cumbria Social Services Inspectorate.* Carlisle: Cumbria Social Services.

Bibliography

Cumbria Social Services (1991) *People First*. Carlisle: Cumbria Social Services.

Cumbria Social Services (1993) *Handbook for Local Authority Managers and Inspectors*. Carlisle: Cumbria Social Services.

Davies, B. and Challis, D. (1986) *Matching Resources to Needs in Community Care*. Aldershot: Gower.

Department of Health (1989) *Homes are for Living In*. London: HMSO.

Department of Health (1990a) *Guidance on Standards for Residential Homes for People with a Physical Disability*. London: HMSO.

Department of Health (1990b) *Making Sense of Inspection*. London: HMSO.

Department of Health (1991) *Inspecting for Quality: Guidance on Practice for Inspection Units in Social Services Departments and Other Agencies*. London: HMSO.

Department of Health (1992) *Inspecting Social Services*. London: HMSO.

Department of Health (1993a) *Social Services Department Inspection Units: the First Eighteen Months*. London: HMSO.

Department of Health (1993b) *School Life: Pupils' Views on Boarding*. London: HMSO.

Department of Health (1993c) *Deregulation: Residential Care Homes, Private Nursing Homes and Hospitals*. Letter from S.V.Hiller, 3 August, London.

Department of Health (1994a) *Social Services Department Inspection Units: Report of an Inspection of the Work of Inspection Units in Twenty Seven Local Authorities*. London: HMSO.

Department of Health (1994b) *Inspecting Social Services*. LAC (94) 16. London: HMSO.

Department of Health (1994c) *Inspecting Social Services: Practice Guidance*. London: HMSO.

Department of Health (1994d) *Inspection of Boarding Schools (Section 87 Children Act 1989): Draft Guidance*. London: HMSO.

Donabedian, A. (1980) *The Definition of Quality and Approaches to its Assessment*. Michigan: Ann Arbour.

East Cumbria Health Authority (undated) *Nursing Homes - Quality Profile with Reference to the Mentally Ill.*

Erikson, E. (1950) *Childhood and Society.* New York: Norton.

Feek, W. (1988) *Working Effectively.* London: Bedford Square Press.

Gentry, E. (1991) Unpublished study. Warwick.

Gibbs, I. and Sinclair, I. (1992a) 'Checklists: their possible contribution to inspection and quality assurance in elderly people's homes' in Kelly, D. and Warr, B. *Quality Counts: Achieving Quality in Social Care Services.* London: Whiting and Birch.

Gibbs, I. and Sinclair, I. (1992b) 'Residential care for elderly people: the correlates of quality', *Ageing and Society,* 1(2), pp.463-482.

Goffman, E. (1956) *Presentation of Self in Everyday Life.*

Goldberg, M. and Connelly, N. (eds.) (1981) *Evaluative Research in Social Care.* London: Heinemann.

Goldberg, M. and Connelly, N. (1982) *The Effectiveness of Social Care for the Elderly.* London: Heinemann.

Guba, E. and Lincoln, Y. (1989) *Fourth Generation Evaluation,* California: Sage Publications

Howe, D. (1992) *The Quality of Care.* London: HMSO

Hudson B. (1993) 'Inspecting social care: the new evaluative local state?', *Local Government Studies* , 19(1), pp.1-8.

IDC Pursuing Quality (1986) Kings Fund.

Irving, S. (1994) *An Evaluation of the Impact of Cumbria Social Services Inspectorate on Quality of Life in Residential Care Homes for Adults.* Unpublished Report, Carlisle.

Jacobson, H. (1994) Unpublished lecture. Manchester Exchange, Manchester.

James, A. (1992) 'Quality and its social construction by managers in care service organisations', in Kelly, D. and Warr, B. *Quality Counts: Achieving Quality in Social Care Services.* London: Whiting and Birch.

Kelly, D. (1990) 'Quality control', *Social Work Today,* 29 November, p.14.

Kelly, D. and Warr, B. (1992) *Quality Counts:Achieving Quality in Social Care Services.* London: Whiting and Birch.

Bibliography

Kemp, E. (1991) *The Birnam Lifestyle Questionnaire*. Carlisle: Garlands Hospital.

King, R., Raynes, N. and Tizard, J. (1971) *Patterns of Residential Care: Sociological Studies in Institutions for Handicapped Children*. London: Routledge and Kegan Paul.

Kingston, P. (1994) 'An Inspector Calls', *The Guardian*, 31 May.

Lishman, J. (ed.) (1984) *Evaluation*. Research Highlights Number Eight. Aberdeeen: Department of Social Work, University of Aberdeen.

Living Options in Practice Papers (1991) 1,2,3.

Malin, N. (ed.) (1987) *Reassessing Community Care*. Croom Helm.

Miller, E. and Gwynne, C. (1972) *A Life Apart*. London: Tavistock.

Millham, S., Bullock, R. and Cherrett, P. (1975) *After Grace - Teeth*. London: Chaucer.

Norfolk County Council/Age Concern (1988) *Tell Us What It Is Really Like To Be a Resident in Local Authority Care in Norfolk in 1988*. Norfolk: Norfolk County Council.

Peters, T. (1987) *Thriving on Chaos*. New York: Alfred Knopf.

The Quartz System (1992) *A Comprehensive Development Approach to Quality Assurance in Mental Health Services*. Pavilion.

Rickford, F. (1992) 'Home truths', *Social Work Today*, 26 November, pp.16-17.

Ritchie, P. (1992) 'Establishing standards in social care' in Kelly, D. and Warr, B. *Quality Counts: Achieving Quality in Social Care Services*. London: Whiting and Birch.

Social Services Inspectorate (1992) *The Impact of Inspection on Social Services Department Service Managers, Report of a Workshop Held on 14th February 1992*. London: Department of Health.

Theroux, P. (1992) *The Happy Isles of Oceania*. London: Hamish Hamilton.

Thomas, N. (1984) 'Evaluative research and the personal social services' in Lishman, J. (ed.) *Evaluation*. Research Highlights Number Eight. Aberdeeen: Department of Social Work, University of Aberdeen.

Thorpe, D. (1994) *Evaluating Child Protection*. Milton Keynes: Oxford University Press.

Towell, D. (ed.) (1988) *An Ordinary Life in Practice: Developing Comprehensive Community Based Services for People with Learning Disabilities*. London: Kings Fund.

Villeneau, L. (1992) *Housing with Care and Support*. London: MIND/Joseph Rowntree Foundation.

Wagner, G. (1988) *A Positive Choice: Report of an Independent Review of Residential Care*. London: HMSO.

Ward, A. (1993) *Working in Group Care*. Birmingham: Venture.

Wing, H. (1992) 'The role of inspection and evaluation in social care' in Kelly, D. and Warr, B. *Quality Counts: Achieving Quality in Social Care Services*. London: Whiting and Birch.

Winnicott, D. (1964) *The Child, the Family and the Outside Worlds*. Harmondsworth: Penguin.

Appendix

CODE

OF

PRACTICE

CUMBRIA SOCIAL SERVICES INSPECTORATE:
AUTHORITY, FUNCTION, VALUES AND PROCEDURES

**Cumbria Social Services Inspectorate safeguards
and promotes the well being of people in Cumbria
who use social care services**

1. Statutory Responsibilities of Inspection Units

The Registered Homes Act (1984) is the
legislative authority for the requirement that
private and voluntary residential homes (i.e.
independent sector) with four or more residents
must register before they are allowed to
operate. The Registered Homes Amendment Act
(1991) specified that from April 1993 homes with
three residents or less must also register,
though not to the same standards as homes with
four or more residents. The Children Act (1989)
stated (a) that residential homes and schools
are subject to registration and or inspection
and (b) that day care for children under eight
provided for two or more hours per week on 6 or
more occasions per year is subject to
registration and inspection. Local authorities
were required by the National Health Service and
Community Care Act (1989) to establish
inspection units which would also inspect local
authority directly provided residential homes
for adults.

Governmental advice from the Department of
Health's Social Service Inspectorate was that
such units were best placed within social
services departments both to build on skills
already in existence and to reduce the

bureaucracy which would follow from creating new agencies. Cumbria County Council, as nearly all UK local authorities, set up the inspection unit within the social services department.

2. Arms Length

The Inspectorate is required to work at arms length from the management of the department's directly provided services. In Cumbria this criterion is fulfilled by the Head of Quality Assurance & Strategic Advice (QA & SA) who manages the Inspectorate, being accountable to the Director, in a structure which separates inspection from both local authority provided services and commissioning.

3. Even Handedness

The Inspectorate has to be even handed to all sectors in the manner in which it carries out its tasks. The 'even handedness' applies to, first, the setting of common standards and, secondly, to reporting against those standards. In relation to the setting of standards, the task for the Inspectorate and the Inspection Panel (see below, ...) is to determine an appropriate inspection standard. The procedure for reporting against those standards on announced annual inspections is the same in all sectors.

4. Integrity Of The Inspectorate

One of the core responsibilities of the Head of QA & SA, with the Director of Social Services, is to maintain the integrity of the Inspectorate in being arms length and even handed. The Inspection Panel retains an oversight of this.

5. Enforcement Action

Following inspections, the action taken in
the independent and the local authority
sectors differs. In the independent sector
the inspectorate registers homes and day
care facilities for children under eight.
The inspectorate may require owners or
managers to undertake certain work and, in an
extreme case, may take action to remove the
registration. In the local authority sector
requirements are now made in the same way as for
the independent sector and in extreme cases the
matter will be referred to the Special Cases
Sub-Committee or Inspection Panel. Reports of
annual announced inspections of homes in all
sectors are publicly available.

6. Inspection Standard

The **Inspection Standard** is the standard set by
Cumbria Social Services Inspectorate (CSSI) and
approved by Cumbria Social Services Inspection
Panel. The standard is an explicit statement of
what is required of providers of services and
forms a substantial part of the requirement
against which the adequacy will be that which is
judged to be appropriate to life within the
residential home or day care facility. In
setting standards account has to be taken of the
degree of risk to residents and children, the
quality of their life, priorities for
developments and cost. For example a standard
which attempted to eliminate all risks might be
one which stopped residents going out on their
own, obviously not a standard that is sensible
or acceptable. The Inspectorate has to take
account of the technical advice of other
professionals (for example, from Building and
Design, Environmental Health or Fire Officers)
but in, areas for which it has statutory
responsibility, reaches its own judgement in
terms of degree of risk and quality of life.

Where appropriate the standard will relate to
outcome rather than means. For example, an
inspection standard may specify that residents
should be involved in decisions about their
lives rather than specify a particular means of
achieving this.

Where possible the Inspectorate will consult
with both providers and service users in all
sectors about standards. In many, perhaps most,
cases the inspection standard will be one which
the majority of providers accept. However,
there may be occasions when this is not the case
and CSSI, having taken advice, has the authority
to determine its inspection standard.

7. <u>Function</u>

Cumbria Social Services' Inspectorate has three
main tasks:

* To register and/or inspect social services
  provided by the independent sector or the
  local authority as determined by statute or
  Cumbria Social Services Committee's
  Inspection Panel.

* To provide advice on policy and practice for
  Cumbria Social Services.

* To promote good practice within the local
  authority and independent sectors.

CSSI is expected to carry out these tasks to the
highest possible standards within available
resources for all its 'customers'.

'Customers' are taken to be all those who
have a direct interest or involvement in
the work of the CSSI:

- people who live in residential homes or
  schools, or who use day care for children
  under eight;

- the people of Cumbria with concerns about
  the quality of facilities;

- County Councillors;

- owners and managers of those places
  inspected;

- people enquiring about opening a home,
  school or day care facility;

- professionals with whom CSSI has to
  liaise.

8. Requirements for the Inspectorate

It is essential that users and providers of
social services, and the people living in
Cumbria know the details and standards which are
followed by The Cumbria Inspectorate.

These have been drawn up after consulting widely
with the public, councillors, service users and
service providers as well as the Inspectorate
staff themselves.

(a) Information

There will be well-publicised, accurate and
useful information about:
- the function of the Inspectorate;
- rights of users;
- availability of Annual Reports;
- standards to be applied;
- guidance on implementation of those
  standards;
- guidance on choice of service;
- how to get access to the Inspectorate;
- making comment or complaint about CSSI.

The style of the information will be:

- understandable;
- succinct;
- straightforward;
- attractive.

The information and publications will be up to date. They will reflect the views, comments and needs of those making use of them.

(b)   Inspections

The conclusions from inspections and investigations and the decisions from registrations will be based on:

- published standards;
- published guidance;
- published procedures;
- consistent professional opinion of the Inspectorate.

There will be consistency between Inspectorate staff so similar decisions, conclusions and advice will be given.

At inspections, visits or meetings there will be rigorous analysis of what takes place in the service by:

- listening closely to views and comments;
- being observant;
- collecting evidence and data;
- considering the quality of the service for individuals: for those with disabilities, people from different races and cultures, for men and women, girls and boys.

Decisions, conclusions and advice will be:

- impartial;
- honest;
- open, with evidence and justification provided.

Actions will be:

- appropriate;
- systematic.

There will be opportunities for those being registered, inspected or visited to comment or challenge the Inspectorate's decisions or conclusions.

All reports will:

- be straightforward;
- be clear and concise;
- be accurate;
- be relevant;
- specify what is good as well as what is poor.

(c) <u>Cumbria Social Services Inspectorate</u>

The Inspectorate will be accessible, accurate, up to date and efficient in:

- dealing with enquiries or complaints;
- giving advice;
- completing registration;
- carrying out inspections or investigations;
- completing reports.

The Inspectorate will:

- work from a clearly defined value base working to the highest professional and ethical standards, and be at the forefront of professional knowledge;

- work under Cumbria Social Services 'Statement of Direction' and the Equal Opportunities Policy of the County Council;

- promote good practice and challenge bad practice;

- provide a thorough, efficient and economic service.

Test their work against these principles and expect others to judge them by the extent to which their work matches these statements.

(d) <u>Customer</u>

Customers will be given opportunities to comment on and evaluate the work of the Inspectorate; these contributions will be:

- valued;

- receive a response.

Insofar as is possible, CSSI will work in co-operation with its various customers.

9. The Nature of Inspection

At the heart of inspection is the attempt to examine the practice of other people.

CSSI takes the characteristics of a good inspector to be that inspectors have to:

- exercise a high level of professional judgement;

- reach overall conclusions about the quality of the care that is provided;

- base their conclusions on the detail of what they see;

- seek evidence for what is said (they must not rely on or take on trust what they are told);

- search out poor practice;

- use the authority of the post with integrity and humility;

- carry out large numbers of inspections and alert themselves afresh to the importance of what they are doing on each occasion;

- remember not to presume that a place which has been satisfactory on other occasions is necessarily all right on this visit;

- operate within a goldfish bowl, in that their work is under constant scrutiny from people outside and therefore must be of the highest order both in terms of efficiency and of integrity;

- manage the emotional impact of undertaking the investigation of a serious event;

- report on serious events knowing that the report may have implications for the work of others;

- work with an inevitable element of isolation.

10. <u>Location of CSSI; Inspectorate Staff</u>

CSSI has three offices:

- Headquarters;

- Carlisle (covering the districts of Allerdale, Carlisle and Copeland);

- Kendal (covering the districts of Barrow, Eden and South Lakes).

Day to day matters related to individual homes or facilities should be referred to the Carlisle or Kendal offices as appropriate.

The addresses, including phone numbers, for all the offices is contained in the appendix, which also lists all the staff of CSSI.

11. <u>Organisational structures and membership of Inspection Panel and Consultative and Advisory Committees</u>

Inspection Panel and Social Services Committee

The Inspection Panel, a sub committee of the Social Services Committee, ensures that Members have an oversight of inspectorate activity, in the same way as Members on other sub committees oversee the work of other sections. Members receive a Business Plan, determine Cumbrian policy and standards for registration and inspection and set priorities for work. The Inspection Panel makes recommendations to the Social Services Committee.

Consultative Forums and Advisory Committees

Consultative Forums have been designed to get the views of 'customers' of the inspectorate on its work in homes for adults. Two Advisory Committees have been established: (a) for residential schools and children's homes; (b) for day care facilities for children under eight. The views of Forums and Committees are reported to the Inspection Panel, which has oversight of the Inspectorate. They provide the formal machinery for consultation with users of services, providers of services and other interested parties.

12. Liaison with Cumbria Social Services Directly Provided Services

Cumbria Social Services provides the following types of homes and day care which are subject to statutory inspection by CSSI: residential homes for adults and children; day nurseries.

CSSI will inspect these establishments in an even handed way as described earlier.

There are particular links required between CSSI and Cumbria Social Services as Child Protection Agency and Agency for the protection of adults.

Detailed procedures have been written to define the actions to be taken by social workers (under Child Protection procedures) and staff of the CSSI. (see 'The Procedure for the Investigation of Child Abuse involving Allegations against Professional Staff in the Course of their Professional Duties'). These specify:

The procedures for dealing with allegations, including: deciding whether a matter is an allegation of child abuse or bad practice; the information that should be given to management in the home or school, and to governors, when they exist; the system for passing information between Inspectorate and provider and vice versa.

The procedures for considering whether staff should be suspended during an investigation.

The procedures for concluding an investigation including the holding of a case conference.

In relation to allegations of the mistreatment of adults by professional staff, the overriding guidance is contained in a multi agency paper, Mistreatment of Vulnerable Adults.

13. Liaison with Cumbria Social Services Commissioning Section

The Inspectorate does not and should not have any involvement in decisions about the purchase of services. The following information sets out the respective responsibilities of CSSI and the Commissioning Section.

Inspection standards will be determined by the Inspectorate and the Inspection Panel; commissioning standards will be determined by the Head of Commissioning and the Strategic Planning and Resources Sub Committee.

However, it makes sense for the standards for inspection and for purchase to be in harmony if possible, and to that end the Head of QA & SA and the Head of Commissioning meet to examine the extent to which the two sets of standards are compatible.

Once respective specifications have been set for inspection and for purchase, each arm carries the responsibility to ensure that other specifications which are related to its own task are being met.

Thus it is important to emphasise that the responsibility for determining whether or not a contract which has been agreed between purchaser and provider has been met is the responsibility of the Head of Commissioning, not of CSSI.

However, there is a legitimate function for the Inspectorate to comment either on whether particular specifications are being achieved by an individual provider or on whether specifications are useful.

Thus, it is appropriate for the Inspectorate to say to the Head of Commissioning that, in its opinion, a particular specification is not appropriate. The responsibility of determining whether or not to keep that specification as it stands lies with the Head of Commissioning.

Passing Information Between Inspectors and Commissioning Staff: The Commissioning and Inspection functions within Cumbria Social Services are separate and do not have responsibilities for the work of the other. Nevertheless, there are occasions when it is proper for either section to report to the other, for example on the standards of care in individual homes. Procedures have been established, and have been agreed by Cumbria Social Services and health Authority Inspectorates with the Commissioning Section.

The passing of information between Inspectors and Commissioners has a potential difficulty in that informal contacts between

the two sections could influence whether
or not particular providers get business.
Therefore, it is essential that the
procedures are clear, known to all interested
parties, and formal. There must be no use of
informal contact between Inspectorate and
Commissioners to make judgements about the
quality of provision that is being provided
by any particular provider.

As a part of any submission as a potential
provider of services, any establishment will
have to agree that specified information be
made available from the Inspectorate to the
Commissioning Section. We think that the
information that should be available should
be:

> Inspection Reports on any establishment,
> which in any case are available to members
> of the public.

> Any file note or letter which is known to
> the proprietor or manager as a formal
> document and which refers to standards
> within the home and to specific
> recommendations that the Inspectorate
> makes for improvements.

Inspectors (and to a lesser extent
commissioning staff) will have to be sure
that reports and other formal documents are
explicit enough to allow people to
distinguish between the quality of different
places.

It is essential to reiterate that the
responsibility for determining whether a
contract is or is not being met to the level
of specification required remains the
responsibility of the Commissioning function.

In the carrying out of that responsibility, Commissioning staff should have access to agreed formal information from Inspectorate Staff.

There may also be situations in which Commissioning staff, in their capacity of investigating whether or not a particular place is meeting their specifications, discover aspects of practice which they think should be brought to the attention of CSSI. Again the same procedure applies: that is, that information which has been made formally available to the Inspectorate when, in the view of the Commissioner, it is important information for the Inspectorate to have.

In general, the standard for passing information in either direction should be that there is an absolute obligation on either section immediately to pass across information which is of a serious nature. The following is suggested as a means of deciding whether or not urgent action is necessary.

Serious Event

Witness of serious episode such as physical assault of an individual; observation of someone who appears to be suffering from serious neglect or emotional problems; information from a third party which raises serious doubts.

Middle Range Event

Witness or information from a third party of bad care practices, but not ones which put residents at immediate risk

Less Serious Event

Witness or information from a third party
of inadequate care; such episodes may be
cumulative and therefore worrying.

Middle range and less serious events would be
notified in writing.

On all occasions when either inspectorate or
commissioning staff pass such information to the
other, a copy of the information that has been
passed will be passed to the provider of the
service.

Complaints: Complaints may be about:

(i)   the quality of the service,
(ii) a contract being broken, or
(iii) someone not getting a contract.

Quality of Service

The Cumbria Social Services Complaints and
Representations procedures will be examined
for suitability to new systems: the way in
which complaints procedures relate to an
independent service unit; the role of the
line manager of the service; whether a
dissatisfied user may complain first to the
inspectorate and then to the Head of
Commissioning as the person responsible for
purchase.

Breaking of Contract or Not Getting a Contract

Complaints on either of these would go to the
Head of Commissioning on an informal and then
formal basis, and, if not satisfied, to
Director of Social Services.

Clarification of Distinction Between a Residential Care Home and a Nursing Home:

Both Commissioning and Inspectorate staff have interests in ensuring that there are workable distinctions between residential care homes and nursing homes. The Registered Homes Act 1984 determines that there shall be distinct categories for registration of 'residential care home' and 'nursing home'. A residential care home is expected to provide a measure of support with personal care, 'including assistance with bodily functions'. It is an offence for the owner or manager of a residential care home to look after someone who ought to be in a nursing home, though the reverse is not an offence. The legislation fails to make clear the nature of the distinction between residential care and nursing homes. DHSS circular 7/13 suggests that the nursing tasks which may be legitimately carried out within a residential care home are those which are broadly equivalent to what a competent person might provide in her or his own home. Thus, washing, bathing, toileting, changing of certain dressings, administering medicines and calling a doctor fall within the competence of a residential care home. More specialised, therapeutic or invasive nursing, beyond the competence of a lay person, is to take place within a nursing home.

There are considerable difficulties in interpreting this distinction, first because lay people are encouraged to carry out tasks such as routine injections of certain types and secondly because district nurses may carry out nursing tasks in a residential care home. Within Cumbria, the Inspectorates of the Health Authorities and Social Services Department are working on a more detailed local interpretation. A clear specification will also be necessary for the commissioning section of Cumbria Social Services as it sets out specifications for purchase of different types of care.

Appendix

A Procedure for the Continuous Improvement of Services

OUR ───────────> | **MISSION** |

to promote and safeguard the wellbeing of
people in Cumbria who use Social Care services

**TO BE ACHIEVED
BY OUR** ───────────> | **QUALITY POLICY** |

Cumbria Social Services Inspectorate is committed to the achievement
of its mission by implementing a quality system which improves
continuously our methods of operation

We will promote quality by developing standards and procedures based
on learning from:
* service users
* care providers
* Inspectorate staff
* members of the public
* the highest professional and ethical opinion

DESIGNED TO ───────> | **ENSURE** |

people receive the service that has been specified
and are protected from poor practice

people are confident about the work carried out by
the Inspectorate

WHICH WILL ───────> | **RESULT IN** |

the people of Cumbria being more aware of what the
Inspectorate can do to improve quality of services

people calling on us more for advice

Cumbria Inspectorate being in the
forefront of inspection development

Index